Parties

Photography **Nicole Hill Gerulat**

weldon**owen**

Contents

LET'S HAVE A PARTY! 7

Sweetheart Party

19
Granola Hearts with Almonds & Cranberries

20
Grilled Cheese Hearts

21
Creamy Tomato Soup with Pasta Hearts

22
Chocolate-Dipped Strawberries

25
Raspberry Jam Heart Cookies

Garden Tea Party

31
Flower & Fruit Iced Tea

32
Bite-Sized Chocolate Chip Scones

35
Cucumber & Cream Cheese Sandwich Flowers

36
Butterfly-Shaped Pimento Cheese Sandwiches

39
Mini Vanilla Cupcakes with Sparkle Frosting

Springtime Celebration

47
Tie-Dyed Hard-Boiled Eggs

51
Turkey, Avocado & Havarti Pinwheels

52
Broccoli & Cheddar Mini Quiches

53
Honeydew-Mint Agua Fresca

54
Carrot Cake Cupcakes

Shining Stars BBQ

61 Fresh Strawberry Lemonade

62 Mini Corn on the Cob with Lime Butter

65 Chicken Sausage & Veggies Kebabs

66 Ice Cream Sundae Bar

Wake Up to Waffles

75 Waffles with Lots of Toppings

76 Cheesy Scramble with Tomatoes & Basil

79 Yogurt, Berry & Granola Parfaits

80 Monkey Bread with Cinnamon & Pecans

Birthdays & Burgers

87 Build-Your-Own Turkey Sliders

88 Baked Sweet Potato Fries

91 Mac & Cheese Cups

92 Make-Your-Own Milkshakes

95 Chocolate Chip Cookie Birthday Cake

96 White Chocolate-Dipped Pretzels

Spooky & Berry Delicious

103 Spooky Berry Smoothies

104 Cheese Twist "Bones"

106 Veggie Hot Dog "Mummies"

107 Chocolate-Orange Checkerboard Cookies

109 Caramel-Dipped Apple Wedges

Winter Holiday Cookie Party

117 Gingerbread Family Cookies

120 Peppermint Brownie Bites

122 Chocolate-Peanut Butter Drop Cookies

123 Kitchen Sink Cookies

125 Hot Chocolate Cookies

126 Lemon Crinkle Cookies

INDEX **130**

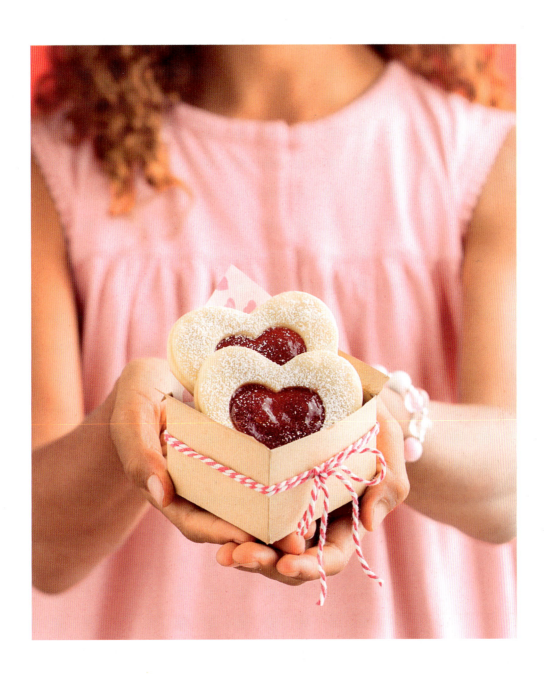

Let's Have a Party!

Who doesn't love an awesome party? Winter, spring, summer, or fall, you can always find a reason to throw a fabulous celebration. Whether you want to host a Valentine's Day Sweetheart Party (page 15) for your very best friends, or invite a bunch of pals to an end-of-year Winter Holiday Cookie Party (page 113), American Girl *Parties* will help you plan everything from snacks to crafts.

Each of the eight party ideas featured in this book is packed with cool tricks that are simple but so much fun. (You'll never guess how many things you can create with cookie cutters!) Make blueberry and watermelon-star skewers for a festive (and healthy) summer barbecue dessert. Or turn your favorite yogurt parfait into an ice pop dipped in granola for a seriously yummy slumber-party breakfast. Don't forget the party favors wrapped in pretty packaging—they can take your gathering from "just fine" to "the best time ever," especially if your friends get to take home what they make. Party time!

Get creative

In these pages, you'll find tons of ideas to throw the perfect party. But think of this book as a jumping-off point that allows you to put your personal stamp on your event. Start by coming up with a theme—we give you eight different fun party plans—and then play around. Use one or all of the recipes we've gathered for that theme, then feel free to mix in some of your own favorites. Go crazy with color and don't be afraid to add a wacky dish to your menu (mint chocolate chip waffles, anyone?). Mix and match the themes or craft ideas and add your own style. Many of the recipes, like Mac & Cheese Cups (page 91) or the Ice Cream Sundae Bar (page 66), will be a hit no matter what type of bash you're hosting. Whatever your party motif—cute and cozy or big and splashy—guests will definitely remember your get-together if you add your own special flair.

Cooking with care

When you see this symbol in the book, it means that you need an adult to help you with all or part of the recipe. Ask for help before continuing.

Adults have lots of culinary wisdom and they can help keep you safe in the kitchen. Always have an adult assist you, especially if your recipe involves high heat, sharp objects, and electric appliances. Be sure to wash your hands before you begin cooking and after touching raw meat, poultry, eggs, or seafood.

Party prep

PLAN YOUR THEME

What kind of party are you hosting? A birthday bash? A movie-night sleepover? A springtime tea party? The time of year and the weather, as well as upcoming holidays, will help you determine the theme, location, colors, and foods to serve.

INVITE FRIENDS

A few weeks before the party, make a guest list and send out invitations designed with the colors and theme of your big bash. Handcrafted notes are super cute, and your friends will love the personal touch. Keep in mind, the bigger the party, the more planning and prep you'll have to do.

STAY ORGANIZED

Checklists are a great way to make sure you remember everything. Include things like shopping for ingredients, making decorations, setting up, and any prep you need to do before the party. Make a to-do list for the day of your get-together so you don't forget anything.

COOK & CRAFT AWAY

Ask friends and family to help you make table decorations, party favors, and other crafty things a few days before the big day. Make sure your menu includes both sweet and savory food. Prepare dishes that can be made ahead so you have time to enjoy all the fun.

The most important thing to remember when hosting a party is to have fun!

Sweetheart Party

On Valentine's Day, you can never have enough red, white, and pink—especially when it comes to party favors and decorations. Share the love with heart-shaped everything and sweet strawberries dipped in chocolate and sprinkles. Grilled Cheese Hearts (page 20) and Creamy Tomato Soup with Pasta Hearts (page 21) make the perfect couple. Wrap up some Raspberry Jam Heart Cookies (page 25) in pretty packaging for your friends or classmates.

★ **Give pretty party favor bags**
Fill heart-patterned cellophane bags with heart-shaped treats and tie them with pink ribbons for fun party favors.

★ **Make your own cards**
Press a pencil eraser onto a red or pink ink pad and use it to create homemade heart-art cards or party invites. A stencil makes shaping the hearts easier.

★ **Make a heart garland**
Cut out pairs of hearts and circles from patterned or colored paper and glue together each pair with a long, thin string sandwiched in between. Repeat along the string.

★ **Set out festive straws**
Tie a mason jar or other glass jar with a ribbon and set it next to the drinks. Fill it with patterned paper straws so everyone can help themselves.

Be mine
Share the love with heart-shaped treats, decorations, and favors.

★ **Give boxes of sweet treats**
Your friends (or a secret crush) would love a festive box of goodies, like homemade cookies or granola bars. Find an array of fun holiday-themed boxes at craft stores or decorate your own with cutouts and ribbons.

Granola Hearts with Almonds & Cranberries

These treats are not only fun for a party, they're great for packing in lunches or taking on a picnic. If you love chocolate, add ½ cup semisweet chocolate chips when you mix in the cranberries. Be sure to use unsalted nuts and seeds in this recipe.

 MAKES ABOUT 16 GRANOLA HEARTS

3 tablespoons unsalted butter, plus more for greasing the baking dish

2 cups old-fashioned rolled oats

1 cup raw whole almonds, coarsely chopped

¼ cup raw pumpkin seeds (pepitas)

¼ cup raw shelled sunflower seeds

½ cup dried currants or raisins

½ cup dried cranberries

⅔ cup honey

¼ cup firmly packed light brown sugar

1 teaspoon vanilla extract

½ teaspoon salt

Preheat the oven to 350°F. Butter a 9-by-13-inch baking dish, line it with parchment paper so that the paper extends beyond the rim of the dish, and butter the paper.

On a rimmed baking sheet, combine the oats, almonds, pumpkin seeds, and sunflower seeds. Bake, stirring the mixture once or twice, until golden, about 8 minutes. Remove the baking sheet from the oven and transfer the mixture to a large bowl. Mix in the currants and cranberries. Reduce the oven temperature to 300°F.

In a small saucepan, combine the honey, sugar, butter, vanilla, and salt. Set the pan over medium heat. Bring the mixture to a boil, stirring often, and cook until the butter is completely melted, about 30 seconds. Pour the hot honey mixture over the oat mixture and stir gently until evenly coated. Empty the mixture into the prepared baking dish and let cool slightly. Using dampened hands, press the granola into an even layer.

Bake until the granola is golden around the edges, about 20 minutes. Remove the baking dish from the oven and set it on a wire rack. Let cool for 5 minutes.

Lift the paper with the granola slab from the baking dish and place the slab on a cutting board. Using a 2½-inch metal heart-shaped cookie cutter, cut out granola hearts while the slab is still warm, pressing the mixture into the cookie cutter to mold it into a heart shape. Transfer the hearts to the wire rack and let cool completely.

Grilled Cheese Hearts

What's not to love about crisp, buttery heart-shaped grilled cheese sandwiches? To make these sammies even more satisfying, add a slice of ham or turkey or even a few thin slices of tomato to each one. Serve with the Creamy Tomato Soup with Pasta Hearts.

 MAKES 4 SANDWICHES

8 slices whole-wheat sandwich bread

4 tablespoons unsalted butter, at room temperature

8 sandwich-size Cheddar cheese slices

Spread one side of each bread slice with 1½ teaspoons of butter. Turn 4 bread slices buttered side down and stack 2 cheese slices on each. Top the cheese with another slice of bread with the buttered side facing up.

Use a large heart-shaped cookie cutter—one that is as close as possible to the size of the bread slices—to cut each sandwich into a heart shape. Discard the scraps.

Set a large frying pan over medium heat. Carefully add the sandwiches and cook until golden brown on the bottom, about 3 minutes. Using a wide metal spatula, carefully flip each sandwich and cook until the second sides are golden brown, about 2 minutes.

Transfer the sandwiches to plates and serve right away.

Creamy Tomato Soup with Pasta Hearts

Little cups of creamy tomato soup with tiny pasta hearts are perfect for a Valentine's Day party. If you can't find heart-shaped pasta, use little stars or orzo instead. And if you don't like garlic, just omit it, but don't skip the cream because it makes the soup yummy.

 MAKES 4 TO 6 SERVINGS

⅓ cup heart-shaped pasta

Salt and ground black pepper

1 teaspoon extra-virgin olive oil

3 tablespoons unsalted butter

1 small yellow onion, chopped

1 clove garlic, minced

1 (28-ounce) can diced tomatoes, with juices

¼ cup heavy cream

Fill a medium saucepan three-fourths full of water. Set the pan over high heat and bring the water to a boil. Add 1 teaspoon of salt and the pasta and cook, stirring occasionally, until the pasta is al dente (tender but still firm at the center); check the package directions for the cooking time. Drain the pasta in a colander set in the sink. Drizzle the olive oil onto the pasta and stir until evenly coated. Set the pasta aside.

Add the butter to a large saucepan. Set the pan over medium heat. When the butter has melted, add the onion and garlic and cook, stirring frequently, until the onion is soft and translucent, about 5 minutes. Add the tomatoes with their juices and bring to a boil. Reduce the heat to low and simmer, stirring occasionally, for 20 minutes. Remove the pan from the heat and let the tomato mixture cool until warm, about 30 minutes.

Transfer the tomato mixture to a blender (do this in batches if necessary). Cover and blend until the soup is smooth. Return the soup to the saucepan, stir in the cream and pasta, and bring to a gentle simmer over medium heat. Taste the soup (careful, it's hot!) and season with salt and pepper.

Ladle the soup into bowls and serve right away.

Chocolate-Dipped Strawberries

Chocolate-dipped strawberries are scrumptious, and making them is a super-fun activity for your sweetheart party. Just line up the berries, set out a few bowls of melted chocolate along with a variety of sprinkles, and invite your friends to dip and decorate.

 MAKES ABOUT 24 STRAWBERRIES

STRAWBERRIES

1 cup semisweet chocolate chips

1 tablespoon vegetable shortening

1 pound strawberries, rinsed and dried

DECORATIONS

Multicolored sprinkles or nonpareils

¼ cup white chocolate chips

To dip the strawberries, select a small saucepan and a heatproof bowl that fits snugly on top of the pan. Fill the pan one-third full of water, making sure the water doesn't touch the bottom of the bowl when the bowl is set on top of the pan. Place the saucepan over medium heat. When the water is steaming, add the chocolate chips and shortening to the bowl and place it on the saucepan. Heat, stirring occasionally with a rubber spatula, just until the mixture is melted and smooth. Remove the pan from the heat, but leave the bowl atop the pan to keep the chocolate warm until you are ready to dip.

Line a cookie sheet with parchment paper or waxed paper. Place the bowl of melted chocolate on the work surface. Working one at a time, hold each strawberry by its green stem and dip it into the melted chocolate until it is about three-fourths covered. Let excess chocolate drip back into the bowl, then place the strawberry on the prepared cookie sheet.

To decorate the berries, while the chocolate is still wet, sprinkle the berries with sprinkles, then refrigerate until set. For white chocolate stripes, refrigerate the dipped berries until set. Melt the white chocolate chips the same way that you melted the semisweet chocolate chips. Use a fork to drizzle the melted white chocolate onto the chilled berries, then refrigerate until set.

Transfer the chocolate-dipped berries to a plate and serve. (The berries are best eaten the day they're dipped, but if necessary, loosely cover them with parchment paper or waxed paper and refrigerate overnight.)

Raspberry Jam Heart Cookies

Heart-shaped, jam-filled sandwich cookies with a dusting of powdered sugar are the perfect treat for any celebration, especially a sweetheart party. If you like, bake the cookies a day ahead, store them in an airtight container, and fill them the day of your party.

 MAKES ABOUT 16 COOKIES

2 cups all-purpose flour

½ teaspoon salt

1 cup (2 sticks) unsalted butter, at room temperature

¾ cup powdered sugar, plus extra for dusting the cookies

2 teaspoons vanilla extract

6 tablespoons seedless raspberry jam

In a bowl, whisk together the flour and salt. In the bowl of an electric mixer, beat the butter and powdered sugar on medium speed until smooth. Add the vanilla extract and beat until blended. Scrape down the bowl with a rubber spatula. Add the flour mixture and beat on low until the dough comes together in large clumps. Dump the dough onto a work surface, divide it in half, and press each piece into a disk. Wrap each disk in plastic wrap and refrigerate until firm, at least 40 minutes or up to overnight.

Position 2 racks evenly in the oven and preheat the oven to 325°F. Line 2 cookie sheets with parchment paper. Sprinkle a work surface with flour. Using flour as needed, roll out one dough disk to ¼ inch thick. Using a 2½-inch heart-shaped cookie cutter, cut out as many cookies as you can. Using a 1-inch heart-shaped cookie cutter, cut out the center from half of the cookie hearts. Place the hearts on the prepared cookie sheets, spacing them evenly. Repeat with the second dough disk. Press the scraps together and repeat the process.

Bake the cookies until the edges are lightly browned, rotating the pans halfway through, 12 to 15 minutes. Let cool on a wire rack for 5 minutes, then use a metal spatula to move the cookies directly to the rack to cool completely.

Spread 1 teaspoon of raspberry jam on each heart without a cutout, leaving a ¼-inch border. Put a little powdered sugar in a sieve, dust the hearts with cut-out centers, then place on top of the jam-covered cookies. Dust the small heart cookies with powdered sugar. Serve right away or store in an airtight container at room temperature for up to 3 days.

Garden Tea Party

This party is fit for fairies. Filled with butterflies, flowers, fancy teacups, and sparkles, it's the perfect afternoon event that you can host in the garden or at a nearby park when the weather is really nice. Use pretty, nature-inspired crafts and colors. Put real flowers (cut some fresh roses from the garden) in dainty tea cups for a sophisticated centerpiece that's as easy as 1-2-3. And oodles of bite-sized sweet treats are a must! Your guests will adore mini vanilla cupcakes topped with sparkly frosting and edible butterflies.

⭐ **Set out butterfly straw cutouts** Purchase butterfly-shaped cutouts that you can slip onto paper straws.

⭐ **Use teacups as flower vases** Gather an array of elegant, colorful teacups and use them as mini vases. Cut the stems short on your favorite big, fluffy flowers and pile them in.

⭐ **Get ready to party** Put on your favorite party clothes and add fresh flowers to your hair. Or weave together flower wreaths to wear as colorful crowns.

★ **Decorate with giant paper flowers** Made from multicolored tissue paper, these massive flowers add lots of bright color and pretty frills. Find them online (or make your own).

A toast with tea
Celebrate with your friends in a pretty outdoor setting.

★ **String up butterflies**
Make or purchase big colorful paper butterflies and then string them up from trees or bushes above and all around the table. They also make terrific tabletop centerpieces.

Flower & Fruit Iced Tea

For this jewel-toned herbal refresher, use hibiscus tea, which is made from the petals of red hibiscus flowers and tastes a little like cranberry juice. You can use a hibiscus-berry tea blend instead, if you like. If you like your tea a little sweeter, add more honey.

 MAKES 4 TO 6 SERVINGS

2½ cups water

3 hibiscus tea bags

1 tablespoon honey, plus more to taste

3 or 4 thin slices fresh unpeeled ginger (optional)

2 cups apple juice

Ice for serving

Fresh mint sprigs, for serving

Add the water to a small saucepan. Set the pan over medium-high heat and bring the water to a boil. Turn off the heat and add the tea bags, honey, and ginger (if using). Cover the pan and set aside for 5 minutes.

Carefully remove and discard the tea bags and ginger slices. Pour the tea into a glass pitcher. Stir in the apple juice. Taste the tea and add more honey, if you like.

Add ice to individual glasses and pour in the tea. Garnish each glass with a mint sprig and serve right away.

Bite-Sized Chocolate Chip Scones

No tea party is complete without scones, and these dainty ones are the best because they're studded with chocolate chips. To make regular-sized scones, use a 3-inch cutter and bake them a few minutes longer. Serve the scones with butter and strawberry jam.

 MAKES ABOUT 16 MINI SCONES

2 cups all-purpose flour

3 tablespoons sugar

2½ teaspoons baking powder

¼ teaspoon salt

½ cup (1 stick) cold unsalted butter, cut into 8 chunks

½ cup mini semisweet chocolate chips

1 cup cold heavy cream

Preheat the oven to 400°F. Line a cookie sheet with parchment paper.

In a large bowl, whisk together the flour, sugar, baking powder, and salt. Scatter the butter chunks over the flour mixture and, using a pastry blender or 2 dinner knives, cut the butter into the dry ingredients until the mixture forms coarse crumbs about the size of peas. Stir in the chocolate chips. Pour in the cream and stir with a fork or rubber spatula just until combined.

Sprinkle a clean work surface with flour and turn the dough out onto the floured surface. Using floured hands, pat the dough into a round about ½ inch thick. Using a 1½-inch biscuit cutter, cut out as many rounds of the dough as possible. Gather up the scraps, knead briefly, and pat and cut out more rounds. Place the rounds on the prepared cookie sheet, spacing them apart evenly.

Bake until the scones are golden brown, about 10 minutes. Remove the cookie sheet from the oven and set it on a wire rack. Serve the scones warm or at room temperature.

Sandwich toppers
Use tissue paper pom-pom or flower cupcake toppers to spear your tea sandwiches and add a splash of color.

Cucumber & Cream Cheese Sandwich Flowers

Nothing says "tea party" quite like these classic finger sandwiches. They're so pretty cut into flower shapes, but you can simply slice them, with or without the crusts, into triangles or long rectangles.

 MAKES 4 SANDWICHES

8 slices good-quality whole-wheat or white sandwich bread

½ cup whipped cream cheese

½ small English cucumber, cut into very thin rounds

Spread one side of each slice of bread with 1 tablespoon of the whipped cream cheese. Top 4 of the cream cheese–covered bread slices with the cucumber slices, dividing them evenly. Place the remaining 4 bread slices on top, cream cheese side down, sandwiching the cucumber.

Use a large flower-shaped cookie cutter—one that is as close as possible to the size of the bread slices—to cut each sandwich into a flower shape. Discard the scraps. Serve right away.

Butterfly-Shaped Pimento Cheese Sandwiches

These yummy cheesy sandwiches are super cute when transformed into butterflies, complete with edible antennae! But you can use any shape cutter you like—just be sure that it's about the same size as your slices of bread to keep the amount of waste to a minimum.

 MAKES 4 SANDWICHES

2½ cups shredded orange-colored sharp Cheddar cheese

⅓ cup rinsed and drained finely chopped pimentos or roasted red peppers

½ cup mayonnaise

Pinch of sugar

8 slices good-quality whole-wheat or white sandwich bread

8 matchstick-sized pieces of carrot or celery

 In a medium bowl, stir together the cheese, pimentos, mayonnaise, and sugar until well combined.

Spread the pimento cheese on 4 of the bread slices, dividing it evenly. Place the remaining 4 bread slices on top, sandwiching the pimento cheese. Use a large butterfly-shaped cookie cutter—one that is as close as possible to the size of the bread slices—to cut each sandwich into a butterfly shape. Discard the scraps.

Tuck 2 carrot or celery matchsticks into the pimento cheese at the top center of each butterfly to create "antennae." Serve right away.

Edible butterflies
Decorate cupcakes or cakes with a rainbow of butterflies made from edible wafer paper (available online).

Mini Vanilla Cupcakes with Sparkle Frosting

Decorated with sparkling sugar or other cute sprinkles, these bite-sized cakes look like sweet treats for garden fairies. The pink icing is pretty, but you can leave it white or change it to your favorite color with a few drops of food coloring.

 MAKES 24 MINI CUPCAKES

CUPCAKES

1½ cups all-purpose flour

2 teaspoons baking powder

¼ teaspoon salt

¾ cup (1½ sticks) unsalted butter, at room temperature

¾ cup granulated sugar

3 large eggs

2 teaspoons vanilla extract

FROSTING

½ cup (1 stick) unsalted butter, at room temperature

3 cups powdered sugar, sifted

Pinch of salt

1 teaspoon vanilla extract

3 drops pink food coloring

Pink and white sparkling sugar, for decorating

 To make the cupcakes, preheat the oven to 350°F. Line a 24-cup mini muffin pan with paper or foil liners.

In a medium bowl, whisk together the flour, baking powder, and salt. In a large bowl, using an electric mixer, beat the butter and granulated sugar on medium-high speed until light and fluffy, about 3 minutes. Add the eggs one at a time, beating well on medium speed after adding each one. Turn off the mixer and scrape down the bowl with a rubber spatula. Add the vanilla and beat until combined. Turn off the mixer. Add about one-third of the flour mixture and mix on low speed until just combined. Turn off the mixer. Add about half of the remaining flour and mix on low speed until just combined. Turn off the mixer. Add the remaining flour and mix on low speed until blended. Scrape down the bowl.

Divide the batter evenly among the muffin cups. Bake until a toothpick inserted into the center of a cupcake comes out clean, about 12 minutes. Remove the pan from the oven and set it on a wire rack. Let the cupcakes cool in the pan for 10 minutes, then transfer them to the rack. Let cool completely.

To make the frosting, in a large bowl, using an electric mixer, beat the butter, powdered sugar, and salt on medium-low speed until smooth and creamy, about 2 minutes. Turn off the mixer and scrape down the bowl with a rubber spatula. Add the vanilla and food coloring and beat until the frosting is evenly colored.

Frost the cupcakes and decorate them with the sparkling sugar. Serve.

Springtime Celebration

When the weather warms up, it's time to celebrate. Nothing says "Spring is here!" like pretty pastels. Blue, green, and yellow look really good together, and you can use that color palette in everything from your table to your menu (mint ice cubes, anyone?). If you're throwing an Easter party, dress up hard-boiled eggs in a swirly tie-dyed pattern. Pile your table with cute bunny and bird decorations and mounds of jelly beans and candy eggs. Carry the theme into dessert with Carrot Cake Cupcakes (page 54) topped with cream cheese frosting and an edible bird's nest. And when it's time to say good-bye, seed packets are an awesome way to send your friends home with something special.

★ **Give seed packet party favors** Spring flower and vegetable seed packets tied with twine make great party favors.

★ **Make mint ice cubes** Add tiny mint leaves to an ice cube tray, fill it with water, and freeze to create flavorful ice cubes. They're great in all types of drinks, from sparkling water to agua fresca.

★ **Decorate branches** For a beautiful centerpiece, use wood glue to affix colorful pom-poms and bird-shaped cutouts to natural tree branches. Pots of fresh herbs are also easy ways to decorate the table.

★ **Set out bowls of colorful candy eggs**
An array of pastel-colored candy eggs, jelly beans, and Jordan almonds will add a little sweetness to your spread.

Spring fling
The start of spring is the perfect time for a party.

★ **Set a springtime table**
A pastel color palette for plates, cups, and napkins creates a fresh, springy table setting. Bowls of shredded colored paper make fun "nests" for serving tie-dyed hard-boiled eggs. Cutouts of bunnies with puffy glued-on tails add a playful touch.

Tie-Dyed Hard-Boiled Eggs

Around Easter, dye kits for eggs are easy to find in any supermarket. At other times, you can easily purchase them online. Look for natural dyes made from herbs, vegetables, and fruits, or make your own with ½ cup boiling water, a little vinegar, and food coloring.

 MAKES 12 EGGS

1 dozen large white eggs

1 egg dye kit

Place the eggs in a large saucepan (save the egg carton!) and add enough cold water to cover by about 1 inch. Cover the pan. Set the pan over high heat and bring the water to a boil. As soon as the water boils, turn off the heat and let stand, covered, for 14 minutes. Using a slotted spoon, transfer the eggs to a colander set in the sink. Discard the water in the pan. Rinse the eggs under cold running water. Fill the pan with cold water and add a few handfuls of ice cubes. Let stand until the eggs are cool, then drain again.

Prepare the dyes according to the package instructions, then pour each dye into its own bowl. Cover your work surface with newspapers, and make sure everyone wears old clothes. Line up the bowls on the work surface. Place a baking sheet with a wire rack set atop or inside of it nearby, along with the empty egg carton. Dye each egg a solid color, ideally one of the lighter colors (or leave the egg in the dye only briefly so the color stays muted). Set aside on the wire rack to dry for 15 to 30 minutes.

Using a small fork or spoon, drizzle each egg with contrasting colors. Let the eggs dry on the rack for about 30 minutes, then place in the egg carton. Refrigerate until party time.

Egg decorating
Place a rack over a cookie sheet or baking dish to catch drips. Spoons work great for drizzling dye onto the eggs.

Turkey, Avocado & Havarti Pinwheels

These playful pinwheel-shaped sandwich bites can be made using any type of flour tortilla, but for a fun and colorful presentation, triple the recipe and use three different-colored tortillas.

 MAKES ABOUT 16 PINWHEELS

½ ripe avocado

2 (8-inch) spinach, tomato, or whole-wheat flour tortillas

2 ounces sliced havarti cheese

3 to 4 ounces sliced smoked or roasted turkey

 Preheat the oven to 350°F. If the avocado half contains the pit, use a spoon to scoop out the pit and discard. Carefully peel off the skin, put the flesh in a small bowl, and roughly mash.

Place the tortillas in a single layer on a cookie sheet. Place the cheese on the tortillas, dividing it evenly and tearing it into smaller pieces so it covers the tortilla evenly. Bake until the cheese melts, about 5 minutes.

Remove the cookie sheet from the oven. Transfer the tortillas to a cutting board. Carefully arrange the turkey slices over the cheese, leaving about 1 inch uncovered on one side. Spread the mashed avocado on top of the turkey. Starting on the turkey-covered side opposite the uncovered side, tightly roll up each tortilla into a cylinder (the exposed melted cheese will act as a glue to hold the cylinder together).

Trim off the ends of each cylinder. Discard (or eat!) the ends, and then slice each cylinder crosswise into 8 pinwheels. Serve right away.

Broccoli & Cheddar Mini Quiches

Put these adorable little quiches out on a serving platter and watch your friends and family gobble them up! You can bake these a day in advance, keep them in the fridge, and then warm them up in a 350°F oven for about 5 minutes before serving.

 MAKES 14 MINI QUICHES

1 sheet frozen all-butter pie dough, about 11 inches square, thawed

2 large eggs

2 tablespoons whole milk

⅓ cup finely chopped cooked broccoli

¼ cup finely shredded Cheddar cheese

 Preheat the oven to 400°F. Spray 14 cups of a 24-cup mini muffin pan with nonstick cooking spray.

Lightly sprinkle a clean work surface with flour and place the dough on the floured surface. If the dough is thicker than ⅛ inch, dust your rolling pin with flour and roll out the dough to that thickness. Using a 2½-inch biscuit cutter, cut out as many rounds as possible. You need 14 rounds; if necessary, gather the scraps into a ball, roll out the dough to ⅛ inch thick, and cut out additional rounds. Make sure the dough stays very cold as you work with it; place it in the refrigerator at any time if it gets too soft and warm. Press 1 round into each greased muffin cup. The edge of the dough should be flush with the rim of the cup.

In a large liquid measuring cup, whisk together the eggs and milk. Divide the broccoli evenly among the dough-lined cups, then fill each cup with some of the egg mixture, leaving a little space at the top and dividing it evenly. (If you have leftover filling, use it to fill the unlined cups for quick frittatas.) Top with the cheese, dividing it evenly.

Bake until the quiches are puffy and golden brown, about 20 minutes. Remove the pan from the oven and set it on a wire rack. Let the quiches cool in the pan for about 5 minutes. Carefully run a small knife around the inside edge of each cup and carefully lift out each quiche. Serve warm or at room temperature.

Honeydew-Mint Agua Fresca

Honeydew melon is the base of this refreshing drink that's sure to be a hit at your springtime party. If you love cantaloupe, just swap it out for the honeydew and follow the same instructions in this recipe. Choose a ripe, fragrant melon for the best flavor.

 MAKES 8 TO 12 SERVINGS

1 large, ripe honeydew melon

Juice of 2 lemons, plus more as needed

⅓ cup sugar, plus more as needed

½ cup fresh mint leaves

3 cups cold water

A few handfuls ice cubes

Fresh mint sprigs, for garnish

Cut the honeydew in half. Using a spoon, scrape out and discard the seeds. Scoop out the flesh and put it into a blender; discard the skin. Add the lemon juice and sugar and blend until smooth. Taste the mixture and add a little more lemon juice and sugar if you like. Pour the mixture into a large bowl and add the mint leaves. Cover and set aside in the refrigerator for at least 1 hour or up to 4 hours, to allow the flavors to blend.

When you're ready to serve, pour the melon mixture through a medium-mesh sieve set over a large pitcher. Add the water and ice and stir well. Pour the agua fresca into glasses, garnish each with a mint sprig, and serve right away.

Carrot Cake Cupcakes

What better way to celebrate springtime than with cinnamon-spiced carrot cakes topped with gooey cream cheese frosting? Decorate with "nests" of toasted coconut and jelly beans or malted milk chocolate eggs, or sprinkle with green and orange sprinkles.

 MAKES 18 CUPCAKES

CUPCAKES

2¼ cups all-purpose flour

1½ cups firmly packed light brown sugar

1 tablespoon baking powder

1 teaspoon ground cinnamon

½ teaspoon salt

1½ cups grated carrots

¾ cup vegetable oil

4 large eggs

1½ teaspoons vanilla extract

FROSTING

4 ounces cream cheese, at room temperature

6 tablespoons (¾ stick) unsalted butter, at room temperature

1 teaspoon vanilla extract

2 cups powdered sugar

DECORATIONS

½ cup shredded coconut, toasted

Jelly beans or speckled malted milk chocolate eggs

 To make the cupcakes, preheat the oven to 325°F. Line 18 cups of two standard muffin pans with paper or foil liners.

In a large bowl, whisk together the flour, brown sugar, baking powder, cinnamon, and salt. In a medium bowl, combine the carrots, oil, eggs, and vanilla and stir until blended. Add the carrot mixture to the flour mixture and stir gently just until blended.

Divide the batter evenly among the prepared muffin cups, filling them only three-quarters full. Bake until a toothpick inserted into the center of a cupcake comes out clean, 16 to 18 minutes. Remove the pans from the oven and set them on a wire rack. Let the cupcakes cool in the pans for about 10 minutes, then transfer them to the rack. Let cool completely.

To make the frosting, in a large bowl, using an electric mixer, beat the cream cheese, butter, and vanilla on medium speed until smooth, about 2 minutes. Turn off the mixer and scrape down the bowl with a rubber spatula. Sift the powdered sugar into the bowl, then beat on low speed until blended.

Using a small icing spatula, frost the cupcakes. Sprinkle the icing with the toasted coconut to create "nests," then top each cupcake with three candies so that they look like "eggs." Serve.

Shining Stars BBQ

As soon as summer rolls around, it's time to get festive. Throw an outdoor barbecue in your backyard decorated with stars, stripes, and red-white-and-blue everything. Hang easy-to-make star streamers, and cover straw bales with red blankets for a rustic touch. Fire up the grill and make yummy kebabs on a stick, and keep dessert simple and fun with a make-your-own ice cream sundae bar. Try this neat trick: use star cookie cutters to stamp out shapes from watermelon slices, then slide them on wooden skewers with blueberries. Fresh Strawberry Lemonade (page 61) will keep everyone cool while they're playing party games on the lawn.

★ **Cover straw bales for bench seats** Folding chairs are great, but straw bales are more festive! Cover them with blankets to make seats that are almost as fun as a hayride.

★ **Make shooting-star streamers** Cut out stars from colored paper, then punch two holes on either side. Thread the stars onto a colorful string to make a garland you can hang.

★ **Serve starry skewers** Use a star-shaped cookie cutter to cut sliced watermelon into stars, then thread them with blueberries onto tinseled skewers for a refreshing treat.

★ **Include fun lawn games**
Horseshoe toss, ring toss, and croquet are just some of the lively lawn games you can offer at your party for fun and entertainment.

All-American
Throw a big bash filled with red, white, and blue everything!

★ **Set up a sundae bar**
Nothing says "summer party" like a sundae bar. Your friends and family will line up when you bring out an array of ice creams and toppings; think chocolate sauce, whipped cream, berries, crumbled cookies, and candy.

Fresh Strawberry Lemonade

Spruce up each glass of lemonade by adding a strawberry or lemon garnish! Using a paring knife, cut a slice of lemon halfway through or slit a whole strawberry lengthwise, keeping the top intact, then slide the lemon slice or berry onto the rim of the glass.

 MAKES ABOUT 2 QUARTS

1½ cups fresh lemon juice

1¼ cups superfine sugar

12 strawberries, trimmed

6 cups cold water

Ice, for serving

Thin lemon slices, for garnish (optional)

Put the lemon juice and sugar in a blender and blend until the sugar is dissolved, about 1 minute. Add the strawberries and puree until very smooth, about 1 minute. Pour the mixture through a fine-mesh strainer set over a 3-quart pitcher. Stir in the water, cover, and refrigerate until well chilled.

When ready to serve, stir the lemonade and add plenty of ice and lemon slices (if using).

Mini Corn on the Cob with Lime Butter

Nothing screams "summer" like ears of sweet, fresh corn. Cut into fun, eat-it-with-one-hand pieces, then pierce each piece with a short, sturdy wooden skewer for easy eating. Spread with zesty lime butter, corn on the cob just got better!

 MAKES 12 PIECES

4 ears of corn, husks and silk removed

4 tablespoons (½ stick) salted butter, at room temperature

Finely grated zest of 1 lime

 Cut each ear of corn crosswise into thirds. In a small bowl, stir together the butter and lime zest with a fork until blended.

Fill a large pot two-thirds full of water. Set the pot over high heat and bring the water to a boil. Add the corn to the boiling water and cook until the corn kernels are tender when pierced with a fork, 5 to 7 minutes. Using tongs, carefully transfer the corn to a platter. Serve hot or at room temperature with the lime butter for spreading.

Chicken Sausage & Veggie Kebabs

These colorful kebabs are so much fun at an outdoor party. You can use different veggies, if you like—whole button mushrooms and chunks of sweet bell peppers are also yummy. If you don't have an outdoor grill, you can cook the kebabs on a stovetop grill.

 MAKES 8 KEBABS

4 links smoked chicken-apple sausages (about 12 ounces total and each about 6 inches long)

2 medium zucchini

24 cherry tomatoes

2 tablespoons extra-virgin olive oil

Salt and ground black pepper

Soak eight 10-inch bamboo skewers in water to cover for at least 30 minutes.

Cut each sausage link crosswise into 6 evenly sized pieces, for a total of 24 pieces. Trim the ends of the zucchini and cut each one in half lengthwise, then cut each half crosswise into 6 evenly sized chunks, for a total of 24 pieces.

Thread 3 sausage pieces, 3 zucchini chunks, and 3 cherry tomatoes onto each skewer, alternating them as you go. Place the kebabs in a single layer on a cookie sheet, brush them all over with the olive oil, and sprinkle each one with a pinch of salt and pepper.

Ask an adult to help you prepare a medium-hot fire in a gas or charcoal grill and clean and oil the grill grate. Alternatively, grease a large grill pan or frying pan with cooking spray.

Place the kebabs on the grill grate and cook, occasionally turning the kebabs with grill tongs, until the sausage is browned and the vegetables are tender, 10 to 15 minutes. If using a grill pan, let the pan heat for 3 minutes then carefully add the kebabs in a single layer and cook, occasionally turning, for 10 to 15 minutes. Transfer the kebabs to a platter and serve right away.

Ice Cream Sundae Bar

This is the dessert bar of your dreams. Offer up a few different ice cream flavors and a bunch of fun toppings and listen as your friends scream for ice cream. Set the containers of ice cream in a large bowl of ice or in a small cooler to keep them from melting too fast.

 MAKES 6 SERVINGS

WHIPPED CREAM

1 cup cold heavy cream

1 tablespoon sugar

1 teaspoon vanilla extract

Toppings of your choice (see suggestions below)

¼ cup chopped toasted nuts, such as almonds, peanuts, or pecans

6 cherries

¾ cup hot fudge sauce, chocolate syrup, or caramel topping

2 pints vanilla and/or chocolate ice cream (or use your favorite flavors)

To make the whipped cream, in a bowl using an electric mixer, beat the cream, sugar, and vanilla on low speed until the cream thickens. Increase the speed to medium-high and continue to beat until the cream forms soft peaks. Be careful not to overbeat!

Set out the toppings, whipped cream, nuts, and cherries in bowls. Set out some spoons, too.

Put the hot fudge in a small saucepan. Set the pan over low heat and warm the hot fudge, stirring occasionally, just until it's smooth and pourable. Remove the pan from the heat.

Scoop the ice cream into 6 bowls, dividing it evenly. Top each serving with about 2 tablespoons of hot fudge. Allow your guests to top their sundaes however they like.

Topping ideas

Marshmallow or caramel topping

Graham cracker squares, broken into pieces

Sliced strawberries or bananas

Raspberries

Chocolate candies

Roughly crushed chocolate crème sandwich cookies or chocolate chip cookies

Chocolate or rainbow sprinkles

Wake Up to Waffles!

Any day is a good day for this delicious slumber party! Make breakfast the main event with oodles of waffles and toppings, cheesy scrambled eggs, and yogurt parfaits that turn breakfast into dessert. (For an unexpected morning treat, put yogurt and berries into ice-pop molds for parfait pops.) Cover the breakfast table in craft paper and use chalk to write names or draw doodles. Stick to a pink-and-blue color palette to match the berries. Writing out the morning menu on a chalkboard is a fun way to let your friends know what they're about to enjoy.

★ **Tie your spoons on** Use pretty, colorful ribbons to tie spoons around each yogurt-berry parfait cup.

★ **Make parfait pops** For a breakfast treat, freeze yogurt and berries in ice-pop molds. Once the pops are frozen, remove them from the molds, brush one side with some honey, and dip in granola.

★ **Write your own menu** Set up a small chalkboard on your table or against the wall and write your breakfast menu on the board in chalk.

★ **Draw on the table**
Cover your tabletop with craft paper, taping down the edges for a neat finish. Then put out chalk, crayons and/or markers for everyone to decorate.

Good morning, fun! Get creative with your after-slumber-party breakfast.

★ **Set up a waffle bar**
Waffles are a treat when served with butter and maple syrup, but they reach a whole new level with a fun array of berries, mini chocolate chips, and whipped cream to throw on top!

Waffles with Lots of Toppings

If you're making waffles for lots of people and want to serve them all at once rather than as each one is ready, set your oven to 250°F and place a baking sheet inside. Put each waffle in the oven as it finishes cooking to keep them warm until ready to serve.

 MAKES 4 TO 6 SERVINGS

2 cups all-purpose flour

1 tablespoon sugar

1 tablespoon baking powder

¼ teaspoon salt

3 large eggs

1½ cups whole milk

6 tablespoons (¾ stick) unsalted butter, melted

Preheat a waffle iron. In a medium bowl, whisk together the flour, sugar, baking powder, and salt. In a large bowl, whisk the eggs until light and frothy, then whisk in the milk and melted butter. While whisking gently, gradually add the flour mixture and mix just until combined. The batter will be lumpy.

When the waffle iron is ready, pour batter over the cooking grid. Close the lid and cook until the steam subsides and the indicator light signals that the waffle is ready, 2 to 4 minutes. Carefully open the iron, transfer the waffle to a serving plate, and serve right away with toppings. Cook the remaining batter in the same way, serving each waffle as it's ready.

Topping ideas

Pure maple syrup

Raspberry jam or orange marmalade

Sliced strawberries

Raspberries and/or blueberries

Sliced pitted peaches or nectarines

Mini chocolate chips

Sweetened ricotta cheese

Whipped Cream (page 66)

Cheesy Scramble with Tomatoes & Basil

These fluffy eggs have all the ingredients of a cheese pizza: tomatoes, basil, and mozzarella. If you prefer your eggs plain, just leave out the tomatoes and basil but keep the cheese, please!

 MAKES 6 SERVINGS

2 teaspoons olive oil

1 cup cherry or grape tomatoes, halved

Salt and ground black pepper

12 large eggs

2 tablespoons chopped fresh basil

1 tablespoon unsalted butter

4 ounces fresh mozzarella cheese, cut into small cubes

Put the olive oil in a large nonstick frying pan. Set the pan over medium heat. Add the cherry tomatoes and cook, stirring occasionally, until hot and beginning to soften, about 2 minutes. Transfer to a bowl, sprinkle with a little salt and pepper, and cover to keep warm.

In a medium bowl, whisk together the eggs, 1 tablespoon of the basil, ¼ teaspoon salt, and ¼ teaspoon pepper until thoroughly blended.

Add the butter to the frying pan that you used to cook the tomatoes. Set the pan over medium-low heat. When the butter begins to foam, add the egg mixture to the pan and cook until it begins to set, about 30 seconds. Stir with a heatproof spatula, scraping the egg on the bottom and sides of the pan and folding it toward the center. Continue to stir in this way until the eggs form moist, soft curds. Stir the mozzarella and tomatoes into the eggs.

Remove the pan from the heat and let stand until the mozzarella starts to melt, about 1 minute. Sprinkle the remaining 1 tablespoon basil over the scramble and serve right away.

Yogurt, Berry & Granola Parfaits

Making your very own granola is a ton of fun, and then using it in pretty parfaits makes it even more special. Bake up an extra batch, put it into plastic gift bags, tie the bags with ribbons, and give them to your friends as party favors.

MAKES 4 PARFAITS

MAPLE GRANOLA

3 cups old-fashioned rolled oats

2 cups coarsely chopped almonds, pecans, and/or walnuts

1 cup shredded dried unsweetened coconut

1 cup raw shelled sunflower seeds

½ cup pure maple syrup, preferably Grade B

½ cup firmly packed light brown sugar

⅓ cup vegetable oil

1 teaspoon ground cinnamon

¾ teaspoon salt

1½ cups raisins

PARFAITS

2 cups vanilla yogurt

1 cup Maple Granola (or store-bought granola)

About 1 cup mixed berries

To make the maple granola, preheat the oven to 300°F. Lightly oil a roasting pan. Add the oats, almonds, coconut, and sunflower seeds to the prepared pan and mix well. In a medium bowl, whisk together the maple syrup, sugar, oil, cinnamon, and salt until the sugar dissolves. Pour the maple mixture over the oat mixture and mix with your hands until the dry ingredients are evenly moistened.

Bake, stirring every 10 minutes and making sure to move the granola from the edges of the pan to the center, until the granola is golden brown and crisp, 45 to 55 minutes. Remove the pan from the oven and set it on a wire rack. Let the granola cool completely in the pan. Stir in the raisins. (The granola can be stored in an airtight container at room temperature for up to 1 month.)

To make the parfaits, have ready 4 parfait glasses or individual bowls. Layer half of the yogurt, granola, and berries into the glasses, in that order and dividing it evenly, then layer the remaining half of the yogurt, granola, and berries. Serve right away.

Monkey Bread with Cinnamon & Pecans

If you don't want to make your own dough, you can use one package of store-bought frozen Parker House–style rolls. Defrost the rolls, use each one as you would a dough piece, and increase the baking time to 30 minutes.

 MAKES 10 TO 12 SERVINGS

DOUGH

½ cup lukewarm (110°F) water

1 package (2½ teaspoons) active dry yeast

½ cup lukewarm (110°F) whole milk

¼ cup granulated sugar

1 teaspoon salt

1 large egg

¼ cup (½ stick) unsalted butter, melted

3 cups all-purpose flour, plus more as needed

½ cup (1 stick) plus 1 tablespoon unsalted butter, melted

½ cup chopped pecans, plus 2 tablespoons finely chopped

1 cup firmly packed light brown sugar

2½ teaspoons ground cinnamon

To make the dough, in the bowl of a stand mixer, combine the water and yeast and let stand until foamy, about 2 minutes. Add the milk, granulated sugar, salt, and egg and whisk until blended. Stir in the melted butter and 2½ cups of the flour. Attach the dough hook to the stand mixer and mix on low speed. With the mixer running, gradually add the remaining ½ cup of flour, then increase the speed to medium and mix until a dough forms and the dough springs back when pressed with a finger, 3 to 4 minutes. The dough should be soft but not sticky; if needed, mix in more flour, 1 tablespoon at a time, to prevent sticking. Place the dough in a lightly oiled bowl and turn to coat its surface with oil. Cover with plastic wrap and let rise in a warm place until the dough has doubled in bulk, 1 to 1½ hours.

Meanwhile, using a pastry brush, coat the inside of a 10-inch Bundt pan with the 1 tablespoon of melted butter, then sprinkle the 2 tablespoons of chopped pecans in the bottom of the pan. Put the remaining ½ cup of melted butter in a shallow bowl. In another shallow bowl, mix together the brown sugar, cinnamon, and the remaining ½ cup of chopped pecans and set aside.

Lightly flour a work surface. Turn the dough out onto the floured surface and cut it into golf ball–size pieces. Working with a few pieces at a time, roll the dough balls in the melted butter to coat on all sides, then drop them into the brown sugar mixture and toss to coat.

> **Make ahead**
> *Bake the bread a day in advance, let cool, and wrap in foil. When ready to serve, re-warm it in the oven.*

Place the coated dough pieces in the prepared pan, arranging them in even layers. Loosely cover the pan with aluminum foil. (At this point, you can refrigerate the shaped dough in the pan overnight, covered with foil. Remove from the refrigerator and let stand at room temperature for about 1 hour before baking the bread as directed.)

Preheat the oven to 200°F for only 5 minutes, then turn off the oven. Place the pan in the warm oven and let the dough rise until doubled in bulk, 30 to 60 minutes (be sure to keep an eye on the dough so it doesn't collapse). Remove the pan from the oven and preheat the oven to 375°F.

Uncover the pan and bake until the bread is richly browned on top and a toothpick inserted into the loaf about 2 inches from the outer edge of the pan comes out clean, about 25 minutes. Remove the pan from the oven and set it on a wire rack. Let cool for 5 minutes. Ask an adult to help you place a serving plate upside down on top of the pan and, using oven mitts, hold the plate and pan together while turning them over. Carefully lift off the pan.

Let the bread cool until warm, then serve.

Birthdays & Burgers

What could be better than a big pile of bite-sized burgers and anything-goes milkshakes on your birthday? How about a chocolate chip cookie cake? This is the kind of party where you can go crazy with crafts. Fun paper cones with wacky patterns are perfect for serving Baked Sweet Potato Fries (page 88). Scatter rainbow-colored confetti over the tables, and mix and match bowls of all shapes and sizes to hold a variety of milkshake toppings. White Chocolate–Dipped Pretzels (page 96) are a festive favor idea—top them with colorful sprinkles that match your party theme.

★ **Set up a space to showcase gifts**
Designate a small table or a shelf for gifts, then decorate with colorful streamers or crafts.

★ **Top your milkshakes**
Set out bowls of rainbow sprinkles and colored sugars and invite guests to add some pizzazz to their milkshakes.

★ **Decorate with color**
For a fun, happy atmosphere, decorate with bright, whimsical shapes and colors. Contrasting hues help create a festive look and feel.

★ **Hand out party hats**
To get your guests into the celebratory spirit, hand out fun, colorful party hats. Let everyone choose their favorite color.

Birthday fun
A birthday is the ultimate reason to party, so make sure it's memorable!

★ **Choose a pretty cake stand**
Nearly any kind of cake can look festive and party-ready when placed on a colorful cake stand and surrounded by pretty decorations. Top your cake with sparkly cupcake toppers to add some fun.

Build-Your-Own Turkey Sliders

Set out all of your toppings and condiments before you start cooking the burgers. That way, when the sizzling sliders are ready, your guests can build them right away, while the patties are still warm and juicy and the buns are nice and toasty.

 MAKES 16 SLIDERS

FOR SERVING

Ketchup, mustard, and mayonnaise

Sliced pickles

Sliced tomatoes

Small romaine lettuce leaves

Sliced avocado

SLIDERS

2 pounds ground dark-meat turkey

2 tablespoons ketchup

1 tablespoon Dijon mustard

1 teaspoon salt

¼ teaspoon ground black pepper

16 small Cheddar cheese slices

16 slider buns or dinner rolls, split

 Set out bowls of ketchup, mustard, and mayonnaise and plates of sliced pickles, sliced tomato, lettuce leaves, and sliced avocado.

To make the sliders, in a large bowl, combine the turkey, ketchup, mustard, salt, and pepper. Using clean hands, mix until the meat and seasonings are well combined, then divide the mixture into 16 equal pieces. Form each piece into a patty, making it a little bit larger than the diameter of your buns (the patties will shrink slightly when they cook). Place in a single layer on a baking sheet. Wash your hands with warm, soapy water.

Coat a large grill pan or frying pan with nonstick cooking spray. Ask an adult to help you set the pan over medium-high heat and let the pan heat for about 2 minutes. Carefully place the patties in the pan, adding only as many as will comfortably fit in a single layer; you may need to cook the patties in 2 batches. Cook until browned on the bottoms, about 5 minutes. Using a metal spatula, flip over the patties, place a slice of cheese on each one, and continue to cook until the cheese is melted and the meat at the center of the thickest patty is no longer pink, about 5 minutes longer. Using the spatula, transfer the patties to a warm platter.

Working in batches, place the buns cut side down in the pan and cook until lightly browned, 1 to 4 minutes. Transfer to a separate platter.

Serve the patties and buns along with the toppings of your choice and invite your guests to build their own sliders.

Baked Sweet Potato Fries

A burger party just isn't complete without french fries, but deep-frying is a lot of work. With this recipe, you can make things easier—and a little healthier—by baking up yummy, crispy sweet potato fries. Serve these with ketchup or ranch dressing.

 MAKES 4 SERVINGS

2 pounds orange-fleshed sweet potatoes, peeled

3 tablespoons olive oil

Salt

 Preheat the oven to 425°F. Cut the sweet potatoes lengthwise into ¼-inch-thick planks, then cut the planks lengthwise into ¼-inch sticks.

On a large rimmed baking sheet, toss the sweet potatoes with the olive oil and a large pinch of salt until evenly coated. Spread the potatoes in a single layer.

Bake until the sweet potatoes are tender and golden brown, 20 to 25 minutes. Remove the baking sheet from the oven. Sprinkle the fries with a little more salt and serve right away.

Fun paper cones
Roll colorful patterned paper into a cone shape and tape it to hold it in place, then fill it with fries!

Mac & Cheese Cups

Creamy macaroni and cheese will get lots of cheers from your guests, especially when baked in cute individual cups. Use ½-cup ramekins or custard cups, or even small ovenproof teacups. For extra yumminess, top each with crumbled bacon.

 MAKES 6 SERVINGS

Salt

8 ounces dried elbow macaroni pasta

2 tablespoons unsalted butter

2 tablespoons all-purpose flour

1 cup whole milk

½ cup half-and-half

2 cups shredded white Cheddar cheese

2 tablespoons grated Parmesan cheese

2 tablespoons panko bread crumbs

2 tablespoons crumbled cooked bacon (optional)

Preheat the oven to 425°F. Fill a large saucepan three-fourths full of water. Set the pan over high heat and bring the water to a boil. Add 1 tablespoon of salt and the pasta and cook, stirring occasionally, until almost tender (the noodle should still be very firm at the center), about 2 minutes less cooking time than the package instructs. Drain the pasta in a colander set in the sink, then transfer it to a large bowl.

Add the butter to the same saucepan. Set the pan over medium-high heat. When the butter is melted, add the flour and cook, stirring well, until well combined, 1 to 3 minutes. Slowly whisk in the milk and half-and-half, then bring the mixture to a boil while whisking constantly. Cook, whisking frequently to smooth out any lumps, until the mixture has thickened, 4 to 5 minutes. Remove the pan from the heat. Add a pinch of salt and two-thirds of the Cheddar cheese and whisk until smooth.

Pour the cheese sauce over the pasta and stir until well combined. Divide the pasta mixture among six ½-cup ramekins. Top evenly with the remaining Cheddar cheese and the Parmesan, then sprinkle with the panko and bacon (if using). Place the ramekins on a rimmed baking sheet.

Bake until the tops are lightly browned and the cheese sauce is bubbly, 12 to 16 minutes. Remove the baking sheet from the oven. Let cool for about 5 minutes, then serve.

Make-Your-Own Milkshakes

A tall frothy milkshake is the ideal companion to a burger, and with this recipe, you and your friends can blend up your favorite flavors to wash down your sliders. Don't forget to top each milkshake with a big dollop of whipped cream!

 MAKES 4 TO 6 MILKSHAKES

1 cup whole milk, plus more as needed

2 teaspoons vanilla extract

1 quart vanilla ice cream

Whipped Cream (page 66)

Chocolate or rainbow sprinkles (optional)

Put the milk in a blender, followed by the vanilla and then scoops of the ice cream. Cover and blend until smooth, adding more milk as needed to achieve the consistency you desire.

Pour the milkshake into tall chilled glasses, dividing it evenly. Top each with a dollop of whipped cream, add sprinkles (if using), and serve right away.

Flavor variations

Strawberry: Add ⅓ cup strawberry preserves and 2 cups sliced strawberries along with the ice cream and blend as directed.

Chocolate: Add ⅓ cup chocolate syrup along with the ice cream and blend as directed.

Vanilla Malted: Add ¼ cup malted milk powder along with the vanilla and blend as directed.

Banana: Add 3 frozen peeled and sliced bananas along with the ice cream and blend as directed.

Choco-Banana: Add ⅓ cup chocolate syrup and 2 frozen peeled and sliced bananas along with the ice cream and blend as directed.

Chocolate Chip Cookie Birthday Cake

A birthday party just isn't a birthday party without a festive cake. This cake is like a giant chocolate chip cookie, so what's not to love? Decorate the cake as suggested, or double the recipe to make two cakes and layer with your favorite chocolate frosting.

 MAKES 8 TO 10 SERVINGS

2 cups all-purpose flour

2 teaspoons baking powder

½ teaspoon salt

¾ cup (1½ sticks) unsalted butter, at room temperature, plus more for greasing the pan

1⅓ cups firmly packed light brown sugar

2 large eggs

1½ teaspoons vanilla extract

1½ cups semisweet chocolate chips

Whipped Cream (page 66)

11 strawberries, hulled

Preheat the oven to 350°F. Grease a 9-inch round cake pan with butter. Sprinkle some flour in the pan and shake and tilt the pan to evenly coat the bottom and sides. Turn the pan upside down and tap out the excess flour.

In a small bowl, whisk together the flour, baking powder, and salt. In a large bowl, using an electric mixer, beat the butter and sugar on medium speed until creamy, about 3 minutes. Turn off the mixer and scrape down the bowl with a rubber spatula. Add the eggs, one at a time, beating on medium speed until blended. Add the vanilla and beat until blended. Turn off the mixer. Add the flour mixture and mix on low speed just until blended. Stir in the chocolate chips. The dough will be very thick. Scrape the dough into the prepared pan and spread it into an even layer.

Bake until a toothpick inserted into the center of the cake comes out with a few crumbs clinging to it, 40–45 minutes. Remove the pan from the oven and set it on a wire rack. Let cool for 30 minutes. Run a paring knife around the inside edge of the pan to loosen the cake. Ask an adult to help you place the rack upside down on top of the pan and, holding the two together, turn them over. Lift off the pan. Place a serving plate upside down on top of the cake and invert the cake right side up onto the plate. Let the cake cool completely.

Mound the whipped cream on top of the cake and spread it evenly over the top. Place 10 strawberries, pointed sides up, around the edge and 1 in the center. Serve right away.

White Chocolate–Dipped Pretzels

White chocolate–dipped pretzels with colorful sprinkles make great party gifts for guests. They're also just super-yummy to eat! If you prefer milk chocolate or dark chocolate, you can use it instead of the white chocolate.

 MAKES 36 TO 40 MINI PRETZELS

4 ounces good-quality white chocolate, chopped

36 to 40 mini pretzels

Rainbow sprinkles or colored sparkling sugar, for decorating

 Line a cookie sheet with wax or parchment paper.

Select a saucepan and a heatproof bowl that fits snugly on top of the pan. Put the chocolate in the bowl. Fill the pan about one-third full of water, making sure the water doesn't touch the bottom of the bowl when the bowl is set on top of the pan. Place the saucepan over medium-low heat. When the water is steaming, place the bowl on top of the saucepan. Heat the chocolate, stirring occasionally with a rubber spatula, until melted and smooth. Don't let the chocolate get too hot, and use pot holders or oven mitts if you need to touch the bowl. Remove the bowl from the saucepan and let the chocolate cool slightly.

Using your fingers, hold a pretzel in the center and carefully dip it into the melted chocolate, completely covering one side. Place the pretzel chocolate-side-up on the prepared cookie sheet and immediately sprinkle it with sprinkles (the chocolate needs to be wet when you decorate so that the sprinkles will stick). Repeat with the remaining pretzels. If the chocolate in the bowl starts to harden, place it over the hot water in the saucepan and stir until it's once again melted and smooth.

Refrigerate the pretzels until the chocolate sets, about 15 minutes. Serve.

Spooky & Berry Delicious

This Halloween, you can throw the most fun—and scariest—party on the block. Your guests will scream with delight when they see all the yummy Halloween-themed goodies, both savory and sweet, that you've cooked up in your cauldron to get them in the spirit. Get your scare on with blood-red smoothies, cheesy "bone" twists, and hot dog "mummies." We go batty for easy-peasy masks, straws, and smoothie wrappers made from black craft paper. And send them running home with treats swallowed up by googly-eyed monster bags.

★ **Make bat sleeves** Cut out bat shapes from black paper, then glue them to coffee cup sleeves that fit snugly on your glasses. Use with smoothies or other party drinks.

★ **Decorate with streamers and string lights** Create a festive party atmosphere with black, white, and orange streamers and lights.

★ **Give festive bags of candy** Load up small cellophane bags with your favorite candies and tie them with ribbons in Halloween colors.

⭐ **Draw scary faces on balloons** Use a permanent black marker to draw spooky faces on a variety of helium-filled balloons. Tie them with colorful ribbons or string.

Boo! Get in the spooky spirit with some of these fun craft ideas.

⭐ **Make monster treat bags** Fold down the tops of colored lunch bags (decorated with patterns, if you like). Glue googly eyes onto each flap, cut out and glue on white "teeth," and clip on two mini clothespins to make silly horns.

Spooky Berry Smoothies

These tangy blood-red smoothies are a sweet treat for a ghoulish get-together. Serve them in tall glasses with festive straws. If you like, swap out frozen raspberries for the strawberries, or strawberry sorbet for the raspberry sorbet.

 MAKES 4 TO 8 SMOOTHIES

1-pound package frozen strawberries

2½ cups cherry, cranberry, or cran-raspberry juice, plus more as needed

1 cup raspberry sorbet

12 ice cubes, plus more as needed

Add all of the ingredients to a blender and blend for 1 to 2 minutes, until smooth, adding more juice or ice as needed to create the consistency you like. You may need to do this in batches, in which case, put half of the ingredients in your blender and proceed as directed, then repeat with the remaining ingredients.

Divide the smoothies between glasses and serve right away.

Cheese Twist "Bones"

These airy, cheesy treats baked into bone shapes are as tasty as they are fun to eat. For the best flavor, look for all-butter puff pastry in the freezer case of a well-stocked market. If you want plain cheese straws, don't cut the ends and leave them as twists.

 MAKES ABOUT 18 "BONES"

1 (14-ounce) package frozen all-butter puff pastry, thawed overnight in the refrigerator

1 large egg, beaten with 1 teaspoon water

½ cup shredded Italian cheese blend or Parmesan

Preheat the oven to 400°F. Line 2 cookie sheets with parchment paper. Sprinkle a work surface with flour. Unfold the puff pastry on the floured surface with a long side near you. It should measure 11 by 14 inches and be ⅛ inch thick. If not, use a rolling pin to roll it to those dimensions.

Brush the pastry sheet with egg wash, then sprinkle the cheese mixture evenly on top. Fold the top third of the pastry down and press gently to seal. Brush the uncovered pastry with egg wash, then fold the bottom third of the pastry up over the egg-washed area. Press to seal.

Using a rolling pin, roll out the pastry into a rectangle measuring about 20 inches long and 5 inches wide. Trim the short edges of the rectangle, then cut the pastry crosswise into 1-inch strips; you should have about 18 strips. Brush the strips with egg wash. Using a paring knife, slit the end of each strip, cutting 1 inch into the pastry and centering the cut on the strip.

Lift up a strip, holding one end in each hand, and turn the ends in the opposite direction to make a twist. Place on one of the prepared cookie sheets, pressing it down so that it stays in place, and pull the slit ends of the strip wide apart so that the shape resembles a bone. Repeat with the remaining strips, placing about 9 "bones" on each cookie sheet and spacing them evenly apart.

Place 1 cookie sheet in the refrigerator and the second cookie sheet in the oven. Bake until the "bones" are nicely browned, about 15 minutes. Remove the cookie sheet from the oven and set it on a wire rack. Bake the second cookie sheet of "bones" in the same way. Let cool to room temperature and serve.

Veggie Hot Dog "Mummies"

Similar to pigs in blankets, these hot dogs are "mummified" in a homemade biscuit dough that bakes up light and fluffy. Dots of ketchup or mustard look like scary mummy eyes. If you prefer, use chicken hot dogs in place of the veggie dogs.

 MAKES 6 SERVINGS

BISCUIT DOUGH

2 cups all-purpose flour, plus more for sprinkling

1 tablespoon baking powder

¾ teaspoon salt

6 tablespoons (¾ stick) cold unsalted butter, cut into small chunks

1 cup whole milk or buttermilk

6 tablespoons shredded Cheddar cheese

6 veggie or chicken hot dogs, each 6 inches long

Ketchup and mustard, for serving

Preheat the oven to 450°F. Line a baking sheet with parchment paper. To make the biscuit dough, in a large bowl, whisk together the flour, baking powder, and salt. Scatter the butter chunks over the flour mixture and, using a pastry blender or 2 dinner knives, cut the butter into the dry ingredients until the mixture looks like coarse crumbs, with small pieces of butter still visible. Pour the milk over the mixture and stir gently with a wooden spoon until clumps form.

Sprinkle a clean work surface with flour. Dump the dough onto the floured surface and knead it a few times until smooth. Using a rolling pin, roll out the dough to a 10-by-15-inch rectangle about ⅓ inch thick, sprinkling flour on the dough as needed to prevent sticking. Cut the rectangle into six 5-inch squares. Sprinkle each dough square with 1 tablespoon of the cheese. Place a hot dog diagonally in the center of each dough square. Lift one uncovered corner of the square up and over the hot dog and press it gently in place. Brush the top of the dough point on the hot dog with water, then lift the opposite corner up and over, wrapping it snugly around the hot dog and the first dough layer, and press gently to help it adhere. Repeat with the remaining hot dogs and dough squares. Place the wrapped hot dogs, seam side up and spaced evenly apart, on the prepared baking sheet.

Bake until the dough is golden brown, 10 to 13 minutes. Remove the baking sheet from the oven and set it on a wire rack. Let cool for a few minutes, then dot two "eyes" on each hot dog with ketchup or mustard. Serve warm.

Chocolate-Orange Checkerboard Cookies

These cute orange and dark brown checkerboard cookies are the colors of Halloween. Prepare the dough logs a day in advance to get a head start. The logs also freeze well in a plastic freezer bag. Just thaw them overnight in the fridge before slicing and baking.

 MAKES ABOUT 30 COOKIES

1 cup all-purpose flour

¼ teaspoon baking powder

⅛ teaspoon salt

½ cup (1 stick) unsalted butter, at room temperature

½ cup sugar

1 large egg, separated

1 teaspoon vanilla extract

1 teaspoon grated orange zest

A few drops orange food coloring

1 ounce semisweet chocolate, melted

2 teaspoons cocoa powder

In a bowl, whisk together the flour, baking powder, and salt. In the bowl of an electric mixer, beat the butter and sugar on medium speed until creamy, about 2 minutes. Add the egg yolk and vanilla and beat until combined. Add the flour mixture and mix on low speed until blended and the dough is smooth. Scrape down the bowl and divide the dough in half. Put one half in a separate bowl and stir in the zest and food coloring. Add the melted chocolate and cocoa to the dough remaining in the bowl and mix on low speed until well blended. Form each portion of dough into a square, wrap separately in plastic wrap, and refrigerate until firm, about 45 minutes.

In a bowl, beat the egg white until foamy. Remove the dough from the refrigerator and cut each into 4 strips. Roll each strip into a ½-inch-thick rope, flouring your hands to prevent sticking. Gently press each rope against the work surface to create squared-off sides. Brush the ropes lightly with egg white. Press a chocolate and orange rope together, then top with 2 ropes, positioning chocolate on the orange and orange on the chocolate. Press to seal. Trim the ends and wrap in plastic wrap. Repeat with the remaining 4 dough ropes. Refrigerate the logs until firm, at least 1 hour or up to overnight.

Position 2 racks evenly in the oven and preheat the oven to 350°F. Line 2 cookie sheets with parchment paper. Cut the dough crosswise into slices ¼ inch thick, then place on the prepared cookie sheets. Bake the cookies until the edges are golden, 8 to 12 minutes. Let cool on the pan on a wire rack for 5 minutes, then use a spatula to move the cookies directly to the rack. Serve.

Caramel-Dipped Apple Wedges

Whole apples covered in caramel look great, but they're difficult to eat. These caramel-dipped apple slices are perfect for a party, and you can enjoy them in just a couple of delicious bites. The pecans are optional, but they add lots of yummy flavor and texture.

 MAKES 16 PIECES

¾ cup chopped pecans or almonds (optional)

1 (11-ounce) bag soft caramel candies

2 tablespoons water

4 apples, quartered and cored

If using the pecans or almonds, preheat the oven to 350°F. Spread the nuts in a single layer on a small cookie sheet. Toast the nuts in the oven, stirring once, until golden and fragrant, about 8 minutes. Remove the baking sheet from the oven and transfer the nuts to a shallow bowl. Set aside.

Line a baking sheet with waxed paper. Unwrap the caramels, place them in a small saucepan, and add the water. Place the pan over medium heat and cook, stirring occasionally, until the caramels have melted and the mixture is smooth, 5 to 7 minutes. Reduce the heat to low.

Hold an apple wedge by one end and dip it in the caramel so that half of it is coated. Let the excess caramel drip back into the pan. If using the nuts, roll the caramel-coated part of the apple in the nuts, pressing gently to help them adhere. Place on the prepared baking sheet. Repeat with the remaining apple wedges. Let stand until the caramel sets, about 10 minutes. Serve, or wrap the apple wedges individually in waxed paper and refrigerate for up to 1 day. Bring to room temperature before serving.

Winter Holiday Cookie Party

Wintry days are the best days to invite friends over for a cookie extravaganza. This silver, white, and blue color scheme is both sweet and sophisticated—plus a touch of sparkle makes it party-rific. Try this trick: cut snowflakes from white coffee filters and string them together to make a pretty garland. Super-cute cookie cutters and big mugs of hot cocoa filled to the rim with marshmallows are a must! And definitely sneak candy canes into as many baked treats as you can, like the ooey-gooey Peppermint Brownie Bites (page 120). Pretty cookie boxes filled with home-baked goodies and tied with shiny ribbons are the ultimate party favors or gifts.

★ **Serve hot drinks** Hot chocolate with mini marshmallows or steaming cups of tea go great with cookies.

★ **Make snowflakes** Fold a white coffee filter in half, then repeat folding 3 times. Cut shapes from the 2 straight sides, then open to reveal a snowflake. String them up with twine to create a garland.

★ **Have boxes and bows for cookies** Gather an array of festive boxes and colorful holiday ribbons and bows so you can create pretty cookie packages for your friends.

★ **Create a forest of paper cone trees** Form white card-stock paper into cone shapes, then wrap and glue decorative paper around each cone. Set them up together like a forest!

Winter sparkle
Warm up cold days by creating a cookie wonderland!

★ **Mix and match cookie shapes** Ask your friends to bring their favorite cookie cutters. Then, use the gingerbread dough (see page 117) to cut out a variety of shapes for baking and decorating.

Gingerbread Family Cookies

Choose a variety of different-shaped cutters for these cookies. Ice them with a piping cone, then decorate with small candies, currants or raisins, mini chocolate chips, and colorful sprinkles and sparkling sugar. After decorating, let the icing dry until it sets.

 MAKES ABOUT 24 COOKIES

GINGERBREAD COOKIES

2¾ cups all-purpose flour

2½ teaspoons baking powder

1 tablespoon ground ginger

1½ teaspoons ground cinnamon

½ teaspoon ground nutmeg

¼ teaspoon salt

½ cup (1 stick) unsalted butter, at room temperature

⅔ cup firmly packed light brown sugar

1 teaspoon vanilla extract

1 large egg

⅓ cup dark molasses

ICING

2 cups powdered sugar

2 tablespoons plus 2 teaspoons warm water

1 tablespoon light corn syrup

To make the gingerbread cookies, in a bowl, whisk together the flour, baking powder, ginger, cinnamon, nutmeg, and salt. In the bowl of an electric mixer, beat the butter and brown sugar on medium speed until creamy, about 3 minutes. Add the vanilla, egg, and molasses and beat until blended. Scrape down the bowl with a rubber spatula. Add the flour mixture and mix on low speed until the dough looks like moist pebbles, about 1 minute. Dump the dough onto a clean work surface, press it together, then divide it in half. Press each mound into a disk, wrap in plastic wrap, and refrigerate for 1 hour.

Position 2 racks evenly in the oven and preheat to 350°F. Line 2 cookie sheets with parchment paper. Sprinkle a work surface with flour. Unwrap 1 chilled dough disk, sprinkle with flour, and roll out the dough to ¼ inch thick. Use more flour as needed so the dough doesn't stick. Cut shapes out of the dough with cookie cutters and set on the prepared cookie sheet. Repeat with the remaining dough, pressing the dough scraps together.

Bake until lightly browned around the edges, rotating the cookie sheets halfway through, 10 to 12 minutes. Let cool on the cookie sheet on a wire rack for about 15 minutes, then use a metal spatula to move the cookies directly to the rack. While the cookies are cooling, bake any remaining cookies the same way. Let the cookies cool completely.

To make the icing, in a bowl, whisk together the powdered sugar, water, and corn syrup until smooth. Decorate the cookies with the icing (see Note above for ideas). Let the icing set for about 30 minutes, then serve.

Peppermint Brownie Bites

Brownies are great for several reasons: they're super easy to make, they're endlessly versatile, and everyone loves them. This version, which is made with two kinds of mint candies, is perfect for the holidays.

MAKES 16 BROWNIE BITES

¾ cup (1½ sticks) unsalted butter, cut into chunks

6 ounces unsweetened chocolate, coarsely chopped

5 or 6 regular-size candy canes, unwrapped

3 large eggs

1½ cups sugar

2 teaspoons vanilla extract

¼ teaspoon salt

1 cup all-purpose flour

16 small chocolate-covered peppermint patty candies, unwrapped

Preheat the oven to 350°F. Spray an 8-inch square baking dish with nonstick cooking spray (you can use a 9-inch square baking dish instead, but the brownies will be thinner).

In a small saucepan, combine the butter and chocolate. Place the pan over medium-low heat and heat the mixture, stirring often, until melted and smooth. Remove from the heat and let cool slightly.

While the chocolate mixture cools, put the candy canes in a large zipper-lock plastic bag. Using a rolling pin, lightly crush them into small chunks. You should have ⅓ to ½ cup of crushed candy canes.

In a large bowl, whisk together the eggs, sugar, vanilla, and salt until blended. Add the chocolate mixture and whisk until blended. Add the flour and whisk slowly just until no lumps remain.

Pour about two-thirds of the batter into the prepared pan and spread it evenly with a rubber spatula. Top with the peppermint patty candies in a single layer. Dollop the remaining brownie batter over the top, gently smoothing into an even layer. Sprinkle the crushed candy canes on top of the batter.

Bake until a toothpick inserted into the center of the brownies comes out with only moist crumbs attached, about 40 minutes. (Be careful not to overbake.) Remove the baking dish from the oven and set it on a wire rack. Let cool completely. Cut the brownies into 16 squares and serve.

Choco-rama
If you like plain brownies, just leave out the 2 types of peppermint candies and bake as directed.

Chocolate-Peanut Butter Drop Cookies

The combination of chocolate and peanut butter is so outrageously yummy in these chewy cookies. You can use either smooth or crunchy peanut butter, depending on your preference. Serve them with tall glasses of cold milk.

 MAKES ABOUT 25 COOKIES

1¼ cups peanut butter, at room temperature

⅔ cup firmly packed light brown sugar

1 large egg

1 teaspoon vanilla extract

½ cup all-purpose flour

About 25 chocolate drop candies, unwrapped

Preheat the oven to 350°F. Line a cookie sheet with parchment paper.

In a large bowl, using an electric mixer, beat the peanut butter and brown sugar on medium speed until blended, about 30 seconds. Turn off the mixer and scrape down the bowl with a rubber spatula. Add the egg and vanilla and beat on medium speed until blended. Turn off the mixer. Add the flour and mix on low speed just until blended.

Scoop up a rounded tablespoonful of dough. Scrape the dough off the spoon into the palm of your other hand and roll the dough into a ball. Place the ball on the prepared baking sheet. Repeat with the remaining dough, spacing the balls about 1 inch apart on the baking sheet.

Bake for 10 to 12 minutes, until the cookies are puffed and appear dry on top. Remove the baking sheet from the oven and set it on a wire rack. Immediately place a chocolate candy, tip pointing up, in the center of each cookie and gently press it down to sink the candy into the cookie. Let cool for 10 minutes, then use a metal spatula to move the cookies directly to the rack. Let cool completely and serve.

Kitchen Sink Cookies

As you might guess from their name, these cookies have it all. Chock-full of oats, chocolate chips, shredded coconut, and toasty almonds, they offer something for everyone. For crispier cookies, press the mounds flat and bake for an additional 2 minutes.

 MAKES ABOUT 3½ DOZEN COOKIES

1 cup slivered almonds

1½ cups all-purpose flour

½ teaspoon baking powder

½ teaspoon baking soda

¼ teaspoon salt

1 cup (2 sticks) unsalted butter, at room temperature

¾ cup firmly packed light brown sugar

½ cup granulated sugar

2 large eggs

1½ teaspoons vanilla extract

2 cups old-fashioned rolled oats

1 cup sweetened shredded coconut

1 (12-ounce) bag semisweet or bittersweet chocolate chips

Position 2 racks evenly in the oven and preheat to 350°F. Spread the almonds on a rimmed baking sheet and toast in the oven, stirring once or twice, until lightly golden, about 8 minutes. Remove the baking sheet from the oven. Let the nuts cool completely.

Increase the oven temperature to 375°F. Line 2 cookie sheets with parchment. In a medium bowl, whisk together the flour, baking powder, baking soda, and salt. In a large bowl, using an electric mixer, beat the butter, brown sugar, and granulated sugar on medium speed until creamy, about 2 minutes. Turn off the mixer and scrape down the bowl with a rubber spatula. Add 1 egg and beat on medium speed until blended. Add the other egg and the vanilla and beat until blended. Turn off the mixer and add the flour mixture. Mix on low speed just until blended. Add the oats and coconut and mix on low speed just until combined. Add the toasted almonds and the chocolate chips and mix just until combined. Scrape down the bowl.

Drop heaping tablespoons of the dough onto the prepared baking sheets, spacing the mounds about 1 inch apart. Bake for 7 minutes, then rotate the cookie sheets. Continue to bake until the edges of the cookies are golden brown, about 6 minutes more. Remove the cookie sheets from the oven and set them on a wire rack. Let cool for 5 minutes, then use a metal spatula to move the cookies directly to the rack. Let the cookies cool completely and serve.

Hot Chocolate Cookies

Do you love a big mug of hot chocolate with marshmallows floating on top? Why not try it in cookie form? These chewy chocolate cookies topped with toasty marshmallows are sure to become your new favorite chocolate treat.

 MAKES ABOUT 26 COOKIES

1½ cups all-purpose flour

½ cup unsweetened cocoa powder, plus more for dusting

¼ cup hot chocolate mix

1 teaspoon baking powder

¼ teaspoon salt

3 large eggs

1⅔ cups sugar

2 teaspoons vanilla extract

4 tablespoons (½ stick) unsalted butter, melted and cooled slightly

1 bag mini marshmallows or 13 regular-size marshmallows, halved crosswise

In a bowl, whisk together the flour, cocoa powder, hot chocolate mix, baking powder, and salt. In the bowl of an electric mixer, beat the eggs, sugar, and vanilla on high speed until light in color and thick, about 3 minutes. Add the butter and beat on medium speed until blended. Scrape down the bowl with a rubber spatula. Add the flour mixture and mix on low speed just until blended. Cover the bowl with plastic wrap and refrigerate for 1 hour.

Position 2 racks evenly in the oven and preheat to 350°F. Line 2 cookie sheets with parchment paper. Scoop up heaping tablespoonfuls of the chilled dough, roll them into balls between the palms of your hands, and place on the prepared cookie sheets, spacing them 2 inches apart.

Bake for 6 minutes, then rotate the cookie sheets. Continue to bake until the cookies are puffed and look dry, 4–6 minutes more. Let cool on a wire rack for 5 minutes, then move the cookies directly to the rack.

Once they are all baked, arrange the cookies in a single layer on one unlined cookie sheet. Position an oven rack 6 inches below the broiler and preheat the broiler. Place a few mini marshmallows on the center of each cookie (or, if using regular-size, place a marshmallow half cut-side-down on the center of each cookie). Broil until the marshmallows are gooey and golden (watch them carefully!). Let cool on a wire rack. Just before serving, put a spoonful of cocoa powder in a fine-mesh sieve and lightly dust the cookies with cocoa.

Lemon Crinkle Cookies

These pretty cookies—a lemon lover's dream—have thin, crisp shells covered in snowy sugar. Inside is a bright burst of edible sunshine and irresistible chewiness. The dough has to chill, so make it the night before your cookie party.

 MAKES ABOUT 28 COOKIES

2 cups all-purpose flour

2 teaspoons baking powder

¼ tsp salt

½ cup (1 stick) unsalted butter, at room temperature

1 cup granulated sugar

1 tablespoon finely grated lemon zest

3 large eggs

3 tablespoons fresh lemon juice

1 teaspoon vanilla extract

½ cup powdered sugar, sifted

In a bowl, whisk together the flour, baking powder, and salt. In a large bowl, using an electric mixer, beat the butter, granulated sugar, and lemon zest on medium speed until creamy, about 2 minutes. Add the eggs one at a time, beating well after adding each one. Turn off the mixer and scrape down the bowl with a rubber spatula. Add the lemon juice and vanilla and beat until blended. Turn off the mixer. Add the flour mixture and mix on low speed just until blended. Cover the bowl with plastic wrap and refrigerate for at least 1 hour or up to overnight.

Position 2 racks evenly in the oven and preheat to 350°F. Line 2 cookie sheets with parchment paper. Put the powdered sugar into a shallow bowl.

Scoop up a tablespoonful of the chilled dough and roll it into a rough ball between the palms of your hands (the dough will be very sticky, so you will need to wash your hands occasionally while you are forming dough balls), then drop it into the powdered sugar and roll until completely covered. Place the balls on the prepared cookie sheets, spacing them about 2 inches apart. Press down on the dough balls to flatten them slightly.

Bake for 7 minutes, then rotate the cookie sheets. Continue to bake until the cookies are cracked and puffed and the edges are just starting to brown, about 6 minutes more. Let cool on a wire rack for 5 minutes, then use a metal spatula to move the cookies directly to the rack. Let cool completely and serve.

Index

Apple Wedges, Caramel-Dipped, 109

B

Baked Sweet Potato Fries, 88
Banana-Choco Milkshakes, 92
Berries. *See also* Strawberries
    Granola Hearts with Almonds
        & Cranberries, 19
    Spooky Berry Smoothies, 103
    Yogurt, Berry & Granola
        Parfaits, 79
Bite-Sized Chocolate Chip Scones, 32
Breads & scones
    Bite-Sized Chocolate Chip
        Scones, 32
    Monkey Bread with Cinnamon
        & Pecans, 80–81
Broccoli & Cheddar Mini Quiches, 52
Brownie Bites, Peppermint, 120
Build-Your-Own Turkey Sliders, 87
Butterfly-Shaped Pimento
    Cheese Sandwiches, 36

C

Cakes & cupcakes
    Carrot Cake Cupcakes, 54
    Chocolate Chip Cookie Birthday
        Cake, 95
    Mini Vanilla Cupcakes with
        Sparkle Frosting, 39
Caramel-Dipped Apple Wedges, 109
Carrot Cake Cupcakes, 54

Cheese
    Broccoli & Cheddar Mini
        Quiches, 52
    Build-Your-Own Turkey Sliders, 87
    Butterfly-Shaped Pimento
        Cheese Sandwiches, 36
    Cheese Twist "Bones," 104
    Cheesy Scramble with Tomatoes
        & Basil, 76
    Cream Cheese Frosting, 54
    Cucumber & Cream Cheese
        Sandwich Flowers, 35
    Grilled Cheese Hearts, 20
    Mac & Cheese Cups, 91
    Turkey, Avocado & Havarti
        Pinwheels, 51
    Veggie Hot Dog "Mummies," 106
Chicken Sausage & Veggie Kebabs, 65
Chocolate
    Bite-Sized Chocolate Chip
        Scones, 32
    Choco-Banana Milkshakes, 92
    Chocolate Chip Cookie Birthday
        Cake, 95
    Chocolate-Dipped Strawberries, 22
    Chocolate Milkshakes, 92
    Chocolate-Orange Checkerboard
        Cookies, 107
    Chocolate-Peanut Butter Drop
        Cookies, 122
    Hot Chocolate Cookies, 125
    Ice Cream Sundae Bar, 66
    Kitchen Sink Cookies, 123
    Peppermint Brownie Bites, 120
    White Chocolate-Dipped
        Pretzels, 96

Coconut
    Carrot Cake Cupcakes, 54
    Kitchen Sink Cookies, 123
    Maple Granola, 79
Cookies & bars
    Chocolate-Orange Checkerboard
        Cookies, 107
    Chocolate-Peanut Butter Drop
        Cookies, 122
    Gingerbread Family Cookies, 117
    Granola Hearts with Almonds
        & Cranberries, 19
    Hot Chocolate Cookies, 125
    Kitchen Sink Cookies, 123
    Lemon Crinkle Cookies, 126
    Peppermint Brownie Bites, 120
    Raspberry Jam Heart Cookies, 25
Corn on the Cob, Mini, with
    Lime Butter, 62
Cranberries & Almonds, Granola
    Hearts with, 19
Creamy Tomato Soup with
    Pasta Hearts, 21
Cucumber & Cream Cheese
    Sandwich Flowers, 35

Drinks
    Flower & Fruit Iced Tea, 31
    Fresh Strawberry Lemonade, 61
    Honeydew-Mint Agua Fresca, 53
    Make-Your-Own Milkshakes, 92
    Spooky Berry Smoothies, 103

E

Eggs
    Cheesy Scramble with Tomatoes
        & Basil, 76
    Tie-Dyed Hard-Boiled Eggs, 47

F

Flower & Fruit Iced Tea, 31
Fresh Strawberry Lemonade, 61
Frosting, Cream Cheese, 54

G

Gingerbread Family Cookies, 117
Granola
    Granola Hearts with Almonds
        & Cranberries, 19
    Maple Granola, 79
    Yogurt, Berry & Granola
        Parfaits, 79
Grilled Cheese Hearts, 20

H

Honeydew-Mint Agua Fresca, 53
Hot Chocolate Cookies, 125
Hot Dog, Veggie, "Mummies," 106

I

Ice cream
    Ice Cream Sundae Bar, 66
    Make-Your-Own Milkshakes, 92

K

Kitchen Sink Cookies, 123

L

Lemonade, Fresh Strawberry, 61
Lemon Crinkle Cookies, 126

M

Mac & Cheese Cups, 91
Make-Your-Own Milkshakes, 92
Maple Granola, 79
Milkshakes, Make-Your-Own, 92
Mini Vanilla Cupcakes with
    Sparkle Frosting, 39
Mint-Honeydew Agua Fresca, 53
Monkey Bread with Cinnamon
    & Pecans, 80–81

N

Nuts
    Caramel-Dipped Apple Wedges, 109
    Granola Hearts with Almonds
        & Cranberries, 19
    Ice Cream Sundae Bar, 66
    Kitchen Sink Cookies, 123
    Maple Granola, 79
    Monkey Bread with Cinnamon
        & Pecans, 80–81

O

Oats
    Granola Hearts with Almonds
        & Cranberries, 19
    Kitchen Sink Cookies, 123
    Maple Granola, 79
Orange-Chocolate Checkerboard
    Cookies, 107

P

Parfaits, Yogurt, Berry & Granola, 79
Pasta
    Creamy Tomato Soup with
        Pasta Hearts, 21
    Mac & Cheese Cups, 91
Peanut Butter-Chocolate Drop
    Cookies, 122
Peppermint Brownie Bites, 120
Pimento Cheese Sandwiches,
    Butterfly-Shaped, 36
Pretzels, White Chocolate-Dipped, 96

Q

Quiches, Broccoli & Cheddar Mini, 52

R

Raspberry Jam Heart Cookies, 25

S

Sandwiches
   Build-Your-Own Turkey Sliders, 87
   Butterfly-Shaped Pimento
      Cheese Sandwiches, 36
   Cucumber & Cream Cheese
      Sandwich Flowers, 35
   Grilled Cheese Hearts, 20
   Turkey, Avocado & Havarti
      Pinwheels, 51
Sausage, Chicken, & Veggie
   Kebabs, 65
Scones, Bite-Sized Chocolate Chip, 32
Sliders, Build-Your-Own Turkey, 87
Smoothies, Spooky Berry, 103
Soup, Creamy Tomato, with
   Pasta Hearts, 21
Spooky Berry Smoothies, 103
Strawberries
   Chocolate-Dipped Strawberries, 22
   Fresh Strawberry Lemonade, 61
   Spooky Berry Smoothies, 103
   Strawberry Milkshakes, 92
Sweet Potato Fries, Baked, 88

T

Tea, Iced, Flower & Fruit, 31
Tie-Dyed Hard-Boiled Eggs, 47
Tomatoes
   Build-Your-Own Turkey Sliders, 87
   Cheesy Scramble with Tomatoes
      & Basil, 76
   Chicken Sausage & Veggie
      Kebabs, 65
   Creamy Tomato Soup with
      Pasta Hearts, 21

Turkey
   Build-Your-Own Turkey Sliders, 87
   Turkey, Avocado & Havarti
      Pinwheels, 51

V

Vanilla
   Mini Vanilla Cupcakes with
      Sparkle Frosting, 39
   Vanilla Malted Milkshakes, 92
Veggie & Chicken Sausage Kebabs, 65
Veggie Hot Dog "Mummies," 106

W

Waffles with Lots of Toppings, 75
White Chocolate-Dipped Pretzels, 96

Y

Yogurt, Berry & Granola Parfaits, 79

weldon**owen**

1150 Brickyard Cove Road, Richmond, CA 94801
www.weldonowen.com

WELDON OWEN INTERNATIONAL
President & Publisher Roger Shaw
SVP, Sales & Marketing Amy Kaneko
Finance & Operations Director Philip Paulick

Associate Publisher Amy Marr
Project Editor Kim Laidlaw

Creative Director Kelly Booth
Associate Art Director Lisa Berman
Original Design Alexandra Zeigler
Senior Production Designer Rachel Lopez Metzger
Production Director Chris Hemesath
Associate Production Director Michelle Duggan
Imaging Manager Don Hill

Photographer Nicole Hill Gerulat
Food Stylists Erin Quon, Pearl Jones
Prop Stylist Veronica Olson
Hair & Makeup Kathy Hill

AMERICAN GIRL *PARTIES*
Conceived and produced by Weldon Owen International
In collaboration with Williams Sonoma, Inc.
3250 Van Ness Avenue, San Francisco, CA 94109

Copyright © 2016 Weldon Owen International, Williams Sonoma, Inc., and American Girl

All rights reserved, including the right of reproduction in whole or in part in any form.

All American Girl marks are owned by and used under license from American Girl.

Printed and bound in the United States

First printed in 2016
10 9 8 7 6 5 4 3 2

Library of Congress Cataloging in Publication data is available

ISBN: 978-1-68188-138-6

ACKNOWLEDGMENTS

Weldon Owen wishes to thank the following people for their generous support to help produce this book: Erica Allen, Lisa Atwood, Maggie Broadbent, Milan Cook, Alexa Hyman, Lily Lovell, Rachel Markowitz, Alexis Mersel, Taylor Olson, Elizabeth Parson, Jennifer Paul, Tatum Quon, Alan Vance, Emely Vertiz, Tamara White, and Dawn Yanagihara

A VERY SPECIAL THANK YOU TO:

Our models: Annabelle Armstrong-Temple, Tallulah Armstrong-Temple, Krischelle Delgado, Lauren Finkelstein, Brooklyn Gorton, Harlan Groetchen, Juliet Hanks, Miranda Harvey, Hannah Hopkins, Hallie Johnson, Tatum Quon, Luke Smith, Delilah Sophia-Siegal, Terrapin Teague, Empress Toney, Colin Tuilevaka, Jr., and Naomi Wang

Our locations: Jill Bergman, The Hawkes Family, Tonya Lemone, The Sorensen Family

Our party supplies: Knot and Bow, Cranky Cakes Shop, Shop Sweet Lulu, Rice

Our clothing: Lali Kids, Tea Collection, Rubies and Gold

★ American Girl®
Cooking

Photography **Nicole Hill Gerulat**

weldon**owen**

COOK UP SOME FUN! 7

Snacks

19
Sweet-n-Salty Popcorn

22
Caprese Kebabs

25
Deviled Eggs

26
Guacamole & Star Chips

31
Griddled Corn Fritters with Lime

32
Lemony Hummus

33
Hot Cheese Dip

34
Fruit & Granola Bars

Soups & Salads

39
Taco Salad

40
Greek Salad Pitas

45
BLT Salad with Avocado

46
Chinese Chicken Salad

47
Chopped Green Salad

48
Chicken Noodle Soup

51
Corn & Potato Chowder

53
Turkey Chili

54
Creamy Tomato Soup with Cheese Toasts

Main Dishes

61
Turkey Sliders with Aioli

62
Fish Sticks & Homemade Tartar Sauce

65
Turkey Club Sandwiches

66
Spiced Beef Tacos

70
Homemade Pizza

75
Rosemary Roast Chicken

76
Fish Tacos with Slaw

80
Baked Chicken Parmesan

84
Spaghetti & Meatballs

88
Teriyaki Chicken & Veggies

91
Hawaiian Chicken Kebabs

92
Ham, Cheese & Roasted Red Pepper Panini

95
Sesame Noodles with Peanut Sauce

96
Baked Penne with Spinach & Cheese

Side Dishes

101
Sweet Potato Chips

102
Cheesy Garlic Bread

105
Sautéed Green Beans with Almonds

106
Creamiest Mashed Potatoes

109
Refried Black Beans

112
Stuffed Baked Potatoes

115
Buttery Peas with Mint

116
Roasted Carrots

119
Roasted Cauliflower

INDEX 120

Cook Up Some Fun!

Being able to cook the food you love to eat is a skill you can have fun with your entire life. You'll be able to make what you want when you want to eat it, and the results will be better for you than food you buy already prepared. With this book as your very own cooking coach, you'll learn how to make delicious snacks, soups, salads, main dishes, and sides not only for yourself but for your friends and family, too!

Any time you work in the kitchen, a parent or other adult should be around to help. But even so, you'll feel a great sense of independence and accomplishment knowing you can create an amazing meal from scratch. You'll also discover that cooking is an activity where you can let your creativity flow. And it's an excellent way to spend time with friends and family.

Whether you want to make yummy treats for a sleepover, cook a special meal for your family, or just have fun and learn some new skills in the kitchen, this book has you covered. Maybe you like to follow a recipe step-by-step so the results are always familiar, or maybe you're the kind of cook who likes to add your own pizzazz to a dish to make it uniquely yours. With these recipes, you can create your own style of cooking and let your personality shine. So go ahead—flip through the pages, bookmark some delish dishes, and get ready to make food that'll have your pals saying "OMG, yum!"

Feast like you mean it!

In these pages, you'll find recipes for irresistible snacks like Sweet-n-Salty Popcorn (page 19), which is perfect for movie night, and Fruit & Granola Bars (page 34), for eating on the go. Lunch gets a fab upgrade with dishes like BLT Salad with Avocado (page 45), Greek Salad Pitas (page 40), and Creamy Tomato Soup with Cheese Toasts (page 54). And for dinner, there's even more yumminess to come! Impress your family and friends with Rosemary Roast Chicken (page 75) or Baked Penne with Spinach & Cheese (page 96). And don't forget the side dishes! Bet you can't eat just one of the Sweet Potato Chips (page 101), and everyone will be saying "Mmmmm" when they try a slice of Cheesy Garlic Bread (page 102).

All of the recipes in this book are ideal for sharing, so host a special dinner, a pizza party, a potluck, a birthday bash, or any kind of get-together that reflects your own style and serve up some of your new favorite dishes.

Cooking with care

When you see this symbol in the book, it means that you need an adult to help you with all or part of the recipe. Ask for help before continuing.

Adults have lots of culinary wisdom, and they can help keep you safe in the kitchen. Always have an adult assist you, especially if your recipe involves high heat, sharp objects, and electric appliances. Be sure to wash your hands before you begin cooking and after touching raw meat, poultry, eggs, or seafood.

Tip-top cooking tips

WATCH THE HEAT
Stovetop burners, hot ovens, boiling water—there's a lot of heat involved in cooking, so it's important to be careful when working in the kitchen. Always use oven mitts when handling hot equipment, and have an adult help you when you're cooking at the stovetop, moving things in and out of the oven, and working with hot liquids or foods.

GET HELP WITH SHARP TOOLS
Soon you'll be chopping, slicing, and mincing, but before you start, make sure an adult is there to help you choose the correct knife (not too big, but not too small either), and be sure to hold the knife firmly at the base. When you're not using the knife, place it somewhere safe so it can't fall on the floor or be reached by younger siblings.

STAY ORGANIZED
Staying organized and paying attention are important cooking skills. Before you fire up the stovetop or oven, read the recipe, including the ingredient list, from start to finish. Then it's time to clear a clean surface and lay out all your cooking tools and ingredients. Once the food starts cooking, be sure to set a timer!

The tools you'll need

The recipes in this book use a few basic cooking tools. There's no need to go out and buy everything all at once—you can collect tools slowly over time, as you try your hand at different recipes and styles of cooking.

★ **An apron** is handy to help keep your clothes tidy when you are cooking.

★ **A baking sheet** is great for cooking food in the oven. The big, flat surface of a baking sheet lets you spread out ingredients like cauliflower or potatoes into a single layer so they cook quickly and evenly. You can line the baking sheet with aluminum foil or parchment paper to prevent food from sticking and to make cleanup a snap.

★ **A food processor** is a small electric appliance that comes with different blades and disks that can slice, chop, purée, and shred ingredients. It can also knead dough. Ask an adult for help when using a food processor and be careful of the sharp blades.

★ **Frying pans and sauté pans** are shallow pans with sloped or straight sides. They can be used for sautéing, stir-frying, and pan-frying. A nonstick pan helps prevent food from sticking and makes cleanup easier.

★ **A ladle** is a long-handled spoon with a cup-like bowl. It's used for serving sauces and soups from deep pots.

★ **Measuring cups and spoons** help you measure your ingredients accurately and easily. Choose graduated sets for dry ingredients and a liquid pitcher for wet ingredients.

★ **Oven mitts or pads** protect your hands from hot pans, oven racks, baking sheets, and baking dishes.

★ **A rubber spatula** is helpful for mixing and for scraping foods out of bowls or pans, like when you transfer hummus from the food processor to a serving bowl. Wide, flat metal spatulas are used to flip food over during cooking.

★ **Saucepans** are deep pots with long handles and lids used for stovetop cooking, such as boiling and simmering. They come in different sizes—small ones hold 1 to 2 quarts, medium ones hold 2 to 3 quarts, and large ones hold about 4 quarts.

Many of the recipes in this book can be customized to include your favorite flavors. Add some personal flair to every dish!

Sweet-n-Salty Popcorn

Two kinds of popcorn—one a little sweet, one a little savory—ensures that everyone gets their favorite snack for your next movie night. Put the popcorn in cute bags or boxes and give each person their own, or just serve it in two bowls and let everyone share!

MAKES 4 SERVINGS

¼ cup canola oil

½ cup popcorn kernels

3 teaspoons salt

¼ cup powdered sugar

1 cup grated Parmesan cheese

3 tablespoons unsalted butter, melted

Pour the canola oil into a large, heavy saucepan. Set the pan over medium heat, add the popcorn, and cover. Cook, shaking the pan often, until you hear kernels popping. Continue to cook, shaking the pan continuously, until the popping slows to 3 to 5 seconds between pops. Remove the pan from the heat, carefully lift off the lid, and divide the popcorn evenly between 2 bowls.

Sprinkle 2 teaspoons of the salt and the powdered sugar over 1 bowl of popcorn. Sprinkle the cheese, butter, and remaining 1 teaspoon salt over the second bowl.

Using clean hands or a large spoon, toss the popcorn in each bowl until well combined. Scoop the popcorn into individual bags or boxes—sweet in one and cheesy in another—and serve right away.

Caprese Kebabs

These cute skewers put all the flavors of caprese salad on a stick! Use multicolored cherry tomatoes for extra fun, and omit the basil if you don't like it. Make sure you toast your bread until it's golden, but not too crisp or the cubes will be hard to skewer.

MAKES 12 KEBABS

12 wooden skewers

Three or four 1-inch-thick slices crusty country-style bread, such as Italian or sourdough

2 tablespoons olive oil

Salt

24 cherry tomatoes

24 small fresh basil leaves

24 small fresh mozzarella balls

 Preheat the oven to 400°F.

Trim the crusts off of the bread and cut the slices into twenty-four 1-inch cubes. Transfer the cubes to a rimmed baking sheet and drizzle with 1 tablespoon of the olive oil. Sprinkle with a little salt, toss to combine, and spread the cubes into an even layer. Bake, stirring once halfway through, until the bread is golden, about 10 minutes. Remove the baking sheet from the oven and let the bread cool completely.

Onto each wooden skewer, thread 2 bread cubes, 2 tomatoes, 2 basil leaves, and 2 mozzarella balls in any order that you like. Place the skewers on a serving dish and drizzle with the remaining 1 tablespoon olive oil. Sprinkle with a little salt and serve right away.

Deviled Eggs

Creamy, tangy deviled eggs are a party favorite. You can personalize them by adding 1 teaspoon pickle relish or grated lemon zest and chopped fresh parsley to the yolk mixture. If you want to get fancy, use a piping bag with a star tip to pipe the yolk mixture.

MAKES 4 SERVINGS

4 large eggs

2 tablespoons mayonnaise

½ teaspoon Dijon mustard

Salt and ground black pepper

Sweet paprika

Gently place the eggs in a medium saucepan and fill the pan with enough cold water to cover the eggs. Set the pan over medium heat. When the water bubbles gently, reduce the heat to low and cook for 15 minutes.

Fill a medium bowl with cold water. Using a slotted spoon, carefully remove the eggs from the pan and place them in the bowl. Let the eggs sit in the water for 10 minutes. Replace with new cold water, if necessary, until the eggs are cool to the touch.

Remove the eggs from the water. Gently tap each one against the work surface and roll it back and forth under your hand, applying light pressure, to crack the shell all over. Carefully peel off the shell.

Cut each egg in half lengthwise. Use a spoon to scoop the yolks out of the egg whites and put them in a small bowl. Place the egg-white halves on a serving platter.

Add the mayonnaise and mustard to the yolks. Use the spoon to mash them to a paste. Season to taste with salt and pepper.

Spoon the yolk mixture into the egg-white halves, dividing it evenly and forming it into a mound. Sprinkle each mound with a pinch of paprika. Serve right away.

Guacamole & Star Chips

Avocados, the main ingredient in guacamole, are not only good for you, they're creamy and scrumptious! This much-loved dip is perfect for a party. If you make your guac in advance, squeeze a little extra lime juice over the top.

MAKES 6 SERVINGS

1 large ripe tomato

3 ripe avocados

Juice of 2 limes

Salt

2 green onions, finely chopped (optional)

½ teaspoon ground cumin (optional)

2 tablespoons chopped fresh cilantro

Tortilla chips for serving (for Star Chips, see Note at right)

Insert the tip of a paring knife into the top of the tomato, just outside of the spot where the stem was attached, and cut around that spot, removing the tough core. Put the tomato on its side and cut it in half crosswise. Use a small spoon to scoop out the seeds from each half. Discard the seeds. Cut each tomato half lengthwise into thin slices. A few at a time, gather the slices into a bundle and cut them crosswise to form small, even cubes. Put the tomatoes in a medium bowl.

Cut the avocados in half lengthwise around the large pits in the centers. Twist the halves in opposite directions to separate them. Using a spoon, scoop out the pits and discard them, and then scoop the avocado flesh out of each half into the bowl with the tomatoes. Add the juice of 1½ limes, ½ teaspoon salt, the green onions (if using), and the cumin (if using) to the avocado mixture. Use a potato masher or fork to mash everything to a chunky paste. Stir in the cilantro. Taste the guacamole and, if you like, stir in more lime juice and salt. Serve with tortilla chips for dipping.

Star Chips Preheat the oven to 350°F. Using a 3-inch star-shaped cookie cutter, cut stars out of six 6-inch corn tortillas (you should get 3 from each tortilla). Lightly grease 2 baking sheets with canola oil, then place the stars on the baking sheets so that they are not overlapping. Bake until brown around the edges, 8 to 10 minutes. Let the chips cool slightly, then transfer to a platter and serve.

Griddled Corn Fritters with Lime

These are made best with fresh corn in the summer, but thawed frozen corn kernels will work, too. For a twist, mix in 1 teaspoon each finely chopped green onion and chopped fresh cilantro and ¼ cup shredded Cheddar cheese with the corn.

MAKES 24 FRITTERS

1½ cups fresh corn kernels (from about 3 ears) or thawed frozen corn kernels, chopped

2 teaspoons fresh lime juice

1 large egg

½ cup whole milk

2 tablespoons unsalted butter, melted and cooled

¾ cup all-purpose flour

¼ cup fine-grind cornmeal

1 teaspoon baking powder

½ teaspoon salt

Canola oil for deep-frying

Lime wedges for serving

In a small bowl, stir together the corn kernels and lime juice (the lime juice actually makes the corn taste sweeter). In a medium bowl, whisk together the egg, milk, and butter until blended. In a large bowl, stir together the flour, cornmeal, baking powder, and salt. Pour the egg mixture into the flour mixture and mix until smooth. Stir in the corn.

Put a wire rack on a large rimmed baking sheet and place the baking sheet near the stove. Pour canola oil into a deep, heavy saucepan to a depth of 1 inch. Set the pan over medium-high heat and warm the oil until it reaches 375°F on a deep-frying thermometer.

Scoop up a heaping tablespoon of batter and very gently add the batter to the hot oil, being careful not to let it splash. Repeat to form more fritters, but don't crowd the pan. Fry the fritters until browned on the bottom, about 2 minutes. Using a slotted spoon, flip the fritters and fry until golden on both sides, puffed, and cooked through, 2 to 3 minutes longer. Using the slotted spoon, transfer them to the wire rack to drain. Fry more fritters in the same way until all of the batter is used up.

Serve right away with lime wedges for squeezing.

Lemony Hummus

Hummus is a snap to make in a food processor. Try puréeing a roasted red pepper or drained oil-packed sun-dried tomatoes with the chickpeas for a tasty twist. Serve hummus with veggie sticks, pita chips, or mini pita breads.

MAKES 6-8 SERVINGS

1 clove garlic, peeled and chopped

One 15-ounce can chickpeas, rinsed and drained

Salt

Water

⅓ cup well-stirred tahini (sesame paste)

1 tablespoon olive oil

Juice of 2 lemons

 Put the garlic, chickpeas, ½ teaspoon salt, and 6 tablespoons water in a food processor and cover. Process the mixture for 1 minute. Turn off the machine and scrape down the sides with a rubber spatula. Replace the lid and purée again until the mixture is smooth, about 1 minute. Add the tahini, olive oil, and lemon juice and blend for another minute. If the mixture is very thick, add more water, 1 teaspoon at a time, and process until well combined. Taste the hummus and blend in more salt if you think it needs it.

Using the rubber spatula, scrape the hummus into a bowl. Serve right away or cover the bowl with plastic wrap and refrigerate for up to 3 days.

Hot Cheese Dip

With two kinds of cheese, this ooey-gooey dip will be the hit of your next party! Swap out crackers for the baguette, and if you like, serve up some sliced apples and steamed broccoli florets for dipping, too.

2 cups shredded Gruyère cheese

2 cups shredded fontina cheese or Swiss cheese

2 tablespoons cornstarch

½ cup low-sodium vegetable or chicken broth

½ cup water

2 tablespoons apple cider vinegar

1 small clove garlic, smashed

1 baguette, cut into cubes, for serving

 Place the cheeses in a 1-gallon zipper-lock plastic bag. Add the cornstarch, seal the bag, and shake until well mixed.

In a medium saucepan, combine the vegetable broth, water, vinegar, and garlic. Set the pan over medium-high heat and bring the liquid to a boil. Reduce the heat to medium, add a handful of the cheese mixture to the broth mixture, and whisk until the cheese is almost fully melted. Repeat with the remaining cheese mixture, adding it handful by handful and whisking until smooth after each addition. After you've added all the cheese, keep whisking until the mixture starts to bubble, about 1 minute longer. Remove and discard the garlic clove.

Transfer the cheese dip to a warmed serving bowl or a fondue pot with a heat source underneath. Serve right away with the baguette slices and with fondue forks for spearing and dunking the bread.

Fruit & Granola Bars

These granola bars taste way better than anything you can buy at the store. Substitute your favorite nuts and dried fruits for the ones listed below, but make sure the nuts you use are raw, not roasted or toasted, since they will cook in the oven.

MAKES 16 BARS

3 tablespoons unsalted butter, plus more for greasing the baking dish

2 cups old-fashioned rolled oats

1 cup raw whole almonds

½ cup raw pumpkin seeds (pepitas)

¼ cup raw sunflower seeds

½ cup dried currants or raisins

½ cup dried cranberries

⅔ cup honey

¼ cup firmly packed light brown sugar

1 teaspoon vanilla extract

¼ teaspoon salt

Preheat the oven to 350°F. Butter a 9-by-13-inch baking dish and line it with parchment paper, extending the paper up and over the sides on two sides. Butter the paper.

On a rimmed baking sheet, combine the oats, almonds, pumpkin seeds, and sunflower seeds. Bake, stirring once or twice, just until golden, about 8 minutes. Remove the baking sheet from the oven and transfer the mixture to a large bowl. Stir in the currants and cranberries and set aside. Reduce the oven temperature to 300°F.

In a small saucepan, combine the butter, honey, sugar, vanilla, and salt. Set the pan over medium heat and bring the mixture to a boil, stirring often. Cook for about 30 seconds, or until the butter is fully melted. Pour the mixture over the oat mixture and stir gently until evenly moistened. Scoop the mixture into the prepared baking dish and let cool slightly.

Using dampened hands, press the mixture into an even layer. Bake until golden around the edges, about 20 minutes. Set the baking dish on a wire rack and let cool for 10 minutes. Using the parchment paper as handles, lift the granola out of the pan and place it directly on the rack. Let cool completely.

Transfer the granola onto a cutting board. To cut the bars, make 3 evenly spaced lengthwise cuts and 3 evenly spaced crosswise cuts across the granola. Serve the bars right away or store them in an airtight container for up to 5 days.

Add pizzazz
Make the guac with star chips (page 26) and serve with this taco-licious salad for a star-rific presentation.

Taco Salad

A towering taco salad with seasoned beef, beans, and cheese makes a hearty and super-tasty lunch. Serve each portion in a bowl-shaped fried corn tortilla for a really festive presentation.

MAKES 4 SALADS

1 pound ground beef

¼ cup taco seasoning mix

⅔ cup water

1 ripe avocado

½ head iceberg lettuce, shredded

2 plum tomatoes, chopped

1 cup canned black beans or pinto beans, rinsed and drained

1½ cups shredded Monterey jack cheese or Cheddar cheese

Your favorite salsa

1 lime cut into 4 wedges

Tortilla chips for serving

Put the ground beef in a large frying pan. Set the pan over medium heat. Cook the meat, breaking up clumps with a wooden spoon, until browned, 8 to 10 minutes. If the beef looks greasy, pour off and discard the fat in the pan. Stir in the taco seasoning and water, raise the heat to high, and bring to a boil. Reduce the heat to low and simmer, stirring often, until the liquid is gone, about 12 minutes.

While the meat is cooking, cut the avocado in half lengthwise around the large pit in the center. Twist the halves in opposite directions to separate them. Using a spoon, scoop out the pit and discard it. Carefully peel the skin off each half, and then cut the avocado into ½-inch cubes.

Divide the lettuce among 4 plates. Top each with equal amounts of the tomatoes, beans, and avocado.

When the meat is done, use a slotted spoon to divide it evenly among the salads, and then sprinkle the cheese on top. Spoon some salsa onto each salad. Serve with the lime wedges for squeezing and tortilla chips alongside.

Greek Salad Pitas

You can turn these stuffed pita sandwiches into wraps by using flour tortillas, Indian naan, or even lavash. Just roll up the filling and take it to go! Try adding some thinly sliced red onion or slivers of red bell pepper.

MAKES **4** SERVINGS

2 regular or whole-wheat pita breads

1 cup chopped romaine lettuce

¼ English cucumber, peeled and chopped

1 large plum tomato, chopped

2 tablespoons chopped pitted black olives (optional)

2 tablespoons crumbled feta cheese or goat cheese

1 tablespoon olive oil

2 teaspoons balsamic or red wine vinegar

Salt

¼ cup Lemony Hummus (page 32) or store-bought hummus

1 cup chopped or shredded cooked chicken

 Preheat the oven to 400°F.

Stack the pita breads and cut them in half. Wrap the halves in aluminum foil. Place in the oven to warm for 5 minutes.

Meanwhile, in a medium bowl, combine the lettuce, cucumber, tomato, olives (if using), and cheese. In a small bowl, whisk together the olive oil and vinegar, season with salt, and then drizzle the mixture over the salad. Using tongs, toss to combine.

Remove the pita breads from the oven and unwrap them. Spread the inside of each pita with 1 tablespoon hummus. Add the chicken, dividing evenly. Spoon the salad inside, dividing it evenly. Serve right away.

BLT Salad with Avocado

This recipe turns a classic sandwich into a chunky, colorful salad. Bacon, lettuce, red and yellow tomatoes, crunchy bread, and avocado are topped off with a creamy, lemony dressing. Yum!

DRESSING

½ cup sour cream

2 tablespoons fresh lemon juice

2 tablespoons grated Parmesan cheese

1 clove garlic, chopped

¼ teaspoon salt

SALAD

8 slices thick-cut bacon

4 thick slices crusty country-style bread, such as Italian or sourdough, cut into cubes

2 tablespoons olive oil

Salt

1 ripe avocado

1 large or 2 medium hearts of romaine lettuce, chopped

1 cup red cherry tomatoes, halved

1 cup yellow cherry tomatoes, halved

 Preheat the oven to 400°F.

To make the dressing, combine the sour cream, lemon juice, Parmesan, garlic, and salt in a food processor. Cover and process until smooth, about 30 seconds.

Arrange the bacon in a single layer on a rimmed baking sheet. Spread the bread cubes in a single layer on a second rimmed baking sheet. Drizzle the olive oil over the bread cubes, sprinkle with salt, and, using clean hands, toss until evenly coated. Put both baking sheets in the oven. Bake the bread cubes until golden brown, about 10 minutes. Remove the baking sheet with the bread from the oven and set aside to cool. Turn the bacon with a spatula, then continue to bake until crisp, 5 to 10 minutes longer. Remove the baking sheet from the oven and transfer the bacon to paper towels to drain. Let cool completely, then chop it into pieces.

Cut the avocado in half lengthwise around the large pit in the center. Twist the halves in opposite directions to separate them. Using a spoon, scoop out the pit and discard it. Carefully peel the skin off each half, and then cut the avocado into small cubes.

In a large salad bowl, combine the lettuce, tomatoes, bacon, bread cubes, and avocado. Drizzle with the dressing and, using tongs or salad servers, toss to combine. Serve right away.

Chinese Chicken Salad

This salad with shredded chicken has a sweet and tangy dressing—and lots of pizzazz! Swap out any of the veggies that you don't like for ones you do. The dressing also makes a terrific sauce for grilled chicken breasts served with steamed rice.

MAKES 4 SERVINGS

DRESSING

2 tablespoons teriyaki sauce

1 tablespoon canola oil

1 tablespoon mayonnaise

1 tablespoon rice vinegar

1 teaspoon toasted sesame oil

1 teaspoon peeled and grated fresh ginger

SALAD

2 tablespoons sliced almonds

2 small boneless, skinless chicken breast halves

4 cups mixed salad greens or shredded lettuce

½ English cucumber, sliced

1 cup sugar snap peas, trimmed and sliced

⅓ cup drained canned mandarin orange slices

¼ cup canned fried chow mein or rice noodles

 To make the dressing, in a small bowl whisk together all of the ingredients until blended.

Put the almonds in a small frying pan. Set the pan over medium heat. Cook, stirring occasionally, until the almonds are lightly browned and smell toasty, 4 to 5 minutes. Transfer to a bowl and let cool completely.

Put the chicken breasts in a small saucepan, add just enough water to cover, and cover with the lid. Set the pan over medium heat and bring to a simmer. Reduce the heat to low and cook until the chicken is opaque when cut into with a knife, 10 to 15 minutes. Using tongs, transfer the chicken to a plate and let cool. When the chicken is cool enough to handle, use your fingers to shred the chicken into bite-sized pieces. Set aside.

In a large serving bowl, combine the salad greens, cucumber, and sugar snap peas. Using tongs or salad servers, toss gently to combine. Scatter the chicken over the top and sprinkle with the almonds and orange slices. Drizzle the dressing over the top and gently toss to combine. Divide the salad among 4 plates, sprinkle each serving with noodles, and serve.

Chopped Green Salad

You'll love this simple green salad with crunchy cucumber, creamy avocado, and garlic dressing. Add cherry tomatoes, grated carrot, or any of your favorite veggies. To make the salad heartier, top it with sliced hard-boiled eggs.

MAKES 6-8 SERVINGS

DRESSING

¾ cup mayonnaise

1 tablespoon whole milk

2½ teaspoons white wine vinegar

1 clove garlic, minced

½ teaspoon sugar

¼ teaspoon salt

SALAD

2 medium cucumbers

2 ripe avocados

2 or 3 large hearts of romaine lettuce, trimmed and chopped

1 cup garlic croutons

To make the dressing, in a small bowl, whisk together the mayonnaise, milk, vinegar, garlic, sugar, and salt. If the dressing is too thick, add a little water to thin it out. Set aside.

To make the salad, peel the cucumbers, cut them in half lengthwise, and use a spoon to scrape out the seeds. Cut the cucumbers into cubes and add them to a large salad bowl. Cut the avocados in half lengthwise around the large pits in the centers. Twist the halves in opposite directions to separate them. Using a spoon, scoop out the pits and discard them. Carefully peel the skin off of each half, and then cut the avocado into cubes.

Add the lettuce to the cucumbers and, using tongs or salad servers, toss to combine. Scatter the avocados on top and sprinkle with the croutons. You can divide the salad among individual bowls and drizzle the dressing on top, or you can drizzle the dressing over the entire salad, toss gently to mix, and serve from the large bowl. Serve right away.

Chicken Noodle Soup

If you or anyone in your family has the sniffles, make this recipe! Nothing is more comforting when you're sick than homemade chicken noodle soup served with a few crackers. It'll chase away the cold—and make the kitchen smell great, too.

MAKES 4 SERVINGS

2 boneless, skinless chicken breast halves

6 cups low-sodium chicken broth

1 medium carrot, peeled, halved lengthwise, and thinly sliced

1 stalk celery, thinly sliced

1½ teaspoons dried thyme, dill, or parsley

Salt

1½ cups wide egg noodles

Crackers, for serving

Place the chicken breasts in a large saucepan and pour in the chicken broth. Set the pan over medium heat and bring to a boil. Reduce the heat to low and simmer, uncovered, until the chicken is opaque throughout when cut into with a knife, 10 to 15 minutes. Turn off the heat. Using tongs, transfer the chicken breasts to a plate and set aside to cool. Leave the pan of broth on the stovetop.

Add the carrot, celery, and thyme into the pan with the broth. Turn on the heat to medium and bring the broth to a gentle simmer. Cook the vegetables, stirring occasionally, until tender, about 10 minutes. Taste the broth (careful, it's hot!) and season with salt if you think it needs some.

When the chicken is cool enough to handle, use your fingers to shred it into bite-sized pieces. Add the shredded chicken to the simmering broth along with the egg noodles. Cook until the noodles are tender but not mushy, about 5 minutes.

Ladle the soup into bowls and serve right away with crackers.

Corn & Potato Chowder

Chunky, creamy chowder (a hearty kind of soup) is perfect for lunch or a dinner. In the summer, use fresh corn since it's in season, but in the winter, use frozen corn kernels. Serve in mugs with thick slices of warm sourdough bread alongside, perfect for dunking.

MAKES 6-8 SERVINGS

2 slices uncooked bacon, finely chopped

½ yellow onion, chopped

1 carrot, peeled and chopped

2 stalks celery, chopped

5 small red new potatoes, peeled and cut into 1-inch pieces

4 cups low-sodium chicken broth

2 cups fresh or frozen corn kernels

1 cup heavy cream

Salt and ground black pepper

Put the bacon in a large saucepan. Set the pan over medium heat and cook the bacon, stirring occasionally, until crisp, about 8 minutes. Transfer to paper towels with a slotted spoon.

Add the onion, carrot, and celery to the pan and cook, stirring occasionally, until tender. Add the potatoes and chicken broth and stir well. Raise the heat to high and bring to a boil, and then reduce the heat to medium-low and simmer, uncovered, until the potatoes are tender, about 20 minutes.

Add the reserved bacon, the corn, and the cream and cook until the corn is tender and the soup is warmed through, about 5 minutes. Taste the chowder (careful, it's hot!) and season with salt and pepper.

Ladle the chowder into soup mugs or bowls and serve right away.

Toppings galore
Sour cream, salsa, and/or chopped cherry tomatoes also make great toppings for this hearty chili.

Turkey Chili

A big steaming bowl of this chili is great on a rainy day. Serve it topped with shredded cheese and a dollop of sour cream, and a slice of warm cornbread alongside. Spoon leftovers over a hot baked potato!

MAKES 6-8 SERVINGS

1 red or green bell pepper

2 tablespoons olive oil

1 small yellow onion, chopped

2 pounds ground dark-meat turkey

3 cloves garlic, minced

¼ cup mild chili powder

Salt and ground black pepper

One 14½-ounce can crushed tomatoes

Two 15-ounce cans kidney beans or pinto beans, rinsed and drained

1 cup low-sodium chicken broth

Shredded cheese, for serving

Sliced green onions, for serving

Cut the bell pepper in half lengthwise. Using a paring knife, remove the stem, seedy core, and ribs and discard. Cut into thin strips. A few at a time, gather the strips into a bundle and cut them crosswise to form small cubes.

Put the olive oil in a large, heavy pot. Set the pot over medium-high heat. Add the bell pepper and onion and cook, stirring occasionally, until softened, about 7 minutes. Add the ground turkey and cook, breaking up clumps with a wooden spoon, until the meat begins to brown, 7 to 8 minutes. Add the garlic, chili powder, ½ teaspoon salt, and ¼ teaspoon pepper and cook, stirring often, for 1 minute. Add the tomatoes, beans, and chicken broth. Bring to a simmer, and then reduce the heat to medium-low. Cook, uncovered and stirring occasionally, until the chili is nice and thick, 8 to 10 minutes. Taste the chili (careful, it's hot!) and adjust the seasoning with salt and pepper.

Ladle the chili into bowls and serve right away with the cheese and green onions.

Creamy Tomato Soup with Cheese Toasts

Tomato-rific soup and warm, melty cheese toasts (open-faced grilled cheese sandwiches) are an awesome pair. If you're taking the soup on the go, crackers and sliced cheese are a great easy-to-pack alternative.

MAKES 6 SERVINGS

SOUP

2 tablespoons unsalted butter

1 tablespoon olive oil

1 small yellow onion, coarsely chopped

2 cloves garlic, minced

One 28-ounce can diced tomatoes

4 cups low-sodium chicken or vegetable broth

½ cup heavy cream

½ teaspoon salt

¼ teaspoon ground black pepper (optional)

CHEESE TOASTS

8 to 12 slices baguette, cut on the diagonal

½ cup shredded Cheddar or Monterey jack cheese

To make the soup, put the butter and oil in a large saucepan. Set the pan over medium heat. When the butter is melted, add the onion and cook, stirring often, until tender and translucent, about 7 minutes. Add the garlic and cook, stirring often, for 2 minutes longer. Add the tomatoes and their juices and the chicken broth. Raise the heat to high and bring to a boil, and then reduce the heat to medium-low and simmer, stirring occasionally, for 20 minutes.

Remove the saucepan from the heat and let the tomato mixture cool slightly. Using an immersion blender, purée the soup in the saucepan until smooth. (If you're using a regular blender, let the soup cool until lukewarm. Working in batches, transfer the soup to the blender and purée until smooth. Pour each batch into a large bowl, and when all of the soup is puréed, pour it back into the saucepan.)

Return the saucepan to medium-low heat and stir in the cream, salt, and pepper, if using. Heat the soup, stirring occasionally, until steaming. Turn off the heat and cover to keep warm.

To make the cheese toasts, preheat the broiler. Place the baguette slices in a single layer on a baking sheet and top them with the cheese, dividing it evenly. Broil the toasts until the cheese is melted, 1 to 2 minutes. Remove the baking sheet from the oven.

Ladle the soup into bowls and serve right away with the cheese toasts.

Put a star on it
For extra fun, cut the cheese slices into stars with a star-shaped cookie cutter!

Turkey Sliders with Aioli

Keep these cute little burgers simple or jazz them up with toppings like sliced avocado or cooked bacon. You can swap Swiss cheese, Monterey jack, or provolone for the Cheddar. And if aioli isn't your thing, use plain mayo.

MAKES 8 SLIDERS

AIOLI

½ cup mayonnaise

2 cloves garlic, minced

¼ teaspoon coarse sea salt

SLIDERS

1 pound ground dark-meat turkey

1 tablespoon ketchup

2 teaspoons Dijon mustard

¼ teaspoon salt

¼ teaspoon ground black pepper

8 slices Cheddar cheese

8 slider buns or dinner rolls, split horizontally

8 small romaine lettuce leaves

8 thin slices tomato

To make the aioli, in a small bowl, whisk the mayonnaise, garlic, and salt until blended. Cover with plastic wrap and refrigerate until you're ready to assemble the sliders.

To make the sliders, in a medium bowl, combine the ground turkey, ketchup, mustard, salt, and pepper. Using clean hands, mix until well combined, and then divide the mixture into 8 equal pieces. Shape each piece into a patty.

Grease a large grill pan or frying pan with cooking spray. Set the pan over medium-high heat. Let the pan heat for 3 minutes, and then carefully add the patties in a single layer. Cook until browned on the bottoms, about 5 minutes. Using a wide metal spatula, flip the patties. Place a slice of cheese on each patty and cook until the cheese is melted and the patties are cooked to your liking, about 5 minutes longer. Using the spatula, transfer the patties to a plate. Place the rolls cut side down in the pan and toast until lightly browned, 1 to 4 minutes.

Spread the toasted sides of the bottom halves of the rolls with aioli. Top each with a lettuce leaf and a slice of tomato, and then top with a patty, cheese side up. Cover with the top halves of the rolls and serve right away.

Fish Sticks & Homemade Tartar Sauce

Homemade fish sticks are our favorites and beat out store-bought any day. Making tartar sauce is easy! Just stir together the mayo, pickles, parsley, capers, and lemon juice in a small bowl.

TARTAR SAUCE

½ cup mayonnaise

¼ cup finely chopped bread-and-butter pickles

1 tablespoon finely chopped fresh flat-leaf parsley

2 teaspoons drained capers, chopped

1 teaspoon fresh lemon juice

FISH STICKS

1½ pounds thick skinless cod or tilapia fillets

1 teaspoon salt

½ cup all-purpose flour

2 large eggs, beaten

1 cup plain dried bread crumbs or panko

3 tablespoons canola oil

 Preheat the oven to 450°F. Prepare the tartar sauce (see Note, above), cover, and set aside.

To make the fish sticks, cut the fish fillets into strips about 1 inch wide and 3 to 4 inches long. Sprinkle the strips all over with the salt.

Put the flour, eggs, and bread crumbs in 3 separate shallow bowls or baking dishes. Line up the bowls in that order from left to right and place a large plate to the right of the bread crumbs.

Coat each piece of fish on all sides with flour and tap off the excess. Dip the flour-coated fish into the eggs, turn to coat, and allow the excess to drip off. Finally, dip the fish into the bread crumbs and turn to coat all sides, pressing so that the bread crumbs stick. Set the breaded fish on the plate.

Pour the canola oil onto a large rimmed baking sheet and use a pastry brush to coat the entire surface. Place the baking sheet in the oven and allow it to heat for 5 minutes. Remove the baking sheet from the oven. Carefully place the breaded fish sticks in a single layer on the hot baking sheet, making sure they don't touch. Bake, turning the fish sticks halfway through with a metal spatula, until crisp and golden, about 12 minutes.

Remove the baking sheet from the oven and transfer the fish sticks to a platter. Serve warm, with the tartar sauce for dipping.

Turkey Club Sandwiches

Like all classic club sandwiches, this one is a double-decker and makes a hefty sandwich that's good to share! For a fun presentation, cut each sandwich into quarters and skewer each section with a frilly toothpick!

MAKES 2 SANDWICHES

3 slices thick-cut bacon

6 slices whole-wheat or multigrain sandwich bread

½ ripe avocado

Mayonnaise

4 slices smoked turkey

2 large lettuce leaves

4 thin slices tomato

Lay the bacon slices in a single layer in a medium frying pan. Set the pan over medium heat and fry the bacon, turning the slices once, until golden and crisp, about 5 minutes. Transfer the bacon to a paper towel–lined plate to drain.

Toast the bread slices in a toaster until golden.

If the avocado half contains the pit, use a spoon to scoop out the pit and discard. Carefully peel off the skin, and then use a dinner knife to cut the avocado into thin slices.

Spread a thin layer of mayonnaise on 1 side of 2 of the toasted bread slices. Arrange the avocado slices on the mayo-coated sides of the bread, dividing them evenly, and then arrange 2 slices of turkey on each. Spread more mayonnaise on each side of another 2 slices of toasted bread and place on top of the turkey. Top each with a lettuce leaf, breaking it to fit on the bread, followed by tomato slices. Break the bacon slices in half and arrange 3 pieces of bacon in a single layer over the tomatoes on each sandwich. Spread more mayonnaise on 1 side of the remaining 2 toasted bread slices. Place each slice, mayo-side down, on top of the bacon and press down gently.

Cut the sandwiches in half on the diagonal. Serve right away.

Spiced Beef Tacos

Plan a fun-filled fiesta and offer up Guacamole & Star Chips (page 26) and these awesomely good tacos. Instead of assembling the tacos yourself, set the toppings out in bowls and let everyone build their own. And make sure to have lots of napkins on hand!

MAKES **6** TACOS

1 tablespoon canola oil

¼ cup chopped yellow onion

1 clove garlic, minced

1 pound ground beef

1 teaspoon ground cumin

2 teaspoons sweet paprika

2 teaspoons mild chili powder

1 teaspoon salt

¼ teaspoon ground black pepper

¼ cup water

Six 8-inch flour or whole-wheat tortillas

1 ripe avocado

1 heaping cup shredded lettuce

2 plum tomatoes, chopped

½ cup shredded Cheddar cheese

 Preheat the oven to 300°F.

Put the canola oil in a large frying pan or sauté pan. Set the pan over medium heat. Add the onion and garlic and cook, stirring occasionally, until softened, about 7 minutes. Add the ground beef and cook, breaking up clumps with a wooden spoon, until browned, 8 to 10 minutes. Spoon off and discard all but 1 tablespoon of the fat in the pan. Add the cumin, paprika, chili powder, salt, and pepper to the beef and stir until combined. Add the water and bring to a simmer, and then reduce the heat to low, cover partially, and cook, stirring occasionally, until most of the water is gone, about 10 minutes. Remove from the heat and cover the pan to keep warm.

Stack the tortillas and wrap them in aluminum foil. Place in the oven to warm for 5 minutes.

While the tortillas are warming, cut the avocado in half lengthwise around the large pit in the center. Twist the halves in opposite directions to separate them. Using a spoon, scoop out the pit and discard it. Carefully peel the skin off each half, and then cut the avocado into small cubes.

Remove the tortillas from the oven and unwrap them. Place 1 tortilla on each of 6 plates. Spoon on the beef filling, dividing it evenly. Sprinkle each with an equal amount of lettuce, tomatoes, avocado, and cheese. Fold each tortilla in half and serve right away.

Veggie tacos
Try swapping out the beef with 2 cans of drained pinto or black beans; just simmer them with the spices and use like beef!

Homemade Pizza

Nothing is more fun than having your best friends over for a homemade pizza party. And the best part is you can each make your dream pizza! You can serve your pizzas with lemonade and a Chopped Green Salad (page 47) for a full meal.

MAKES 12 SMALL PIZZAS

DOUGH

8 cups all-purpose flour

2 packages instant or rapid-rise yeast (4½ teaspoons total)

1 teaspoon salt

3 cups lukewarm water

2 tablespoons olive oil, plus more for oiling the bowl

Cornmeal or semolina for dusting the baking sheets

TOMATO SAUCE

1 tablespoon olive oil

¼ yellow onion, finely chopped

1 clove garlic, minced

One 28-ounce can diced tomatoes, drained

1 tablespoon tomato paste

½ teaspoon dried oregano or basil

Salt and ground black pepper

To make the dough, in the bowl of a stand mixer, whisk together the flour, yeast, and salt. Fit the mixer with the dough hook, add the water and olive oil, and mix on medium speed until a dough forms and pulls cleanly away from the sides of the bowl, about 8 minutes.

Lightly grease a large bowl with olive oil, place the dough in the bowl, and turn the dough over. Cover with plastic wrap and let rise in a warm place until doubled in bulk, about 45 minutes, or in the refrigerator for up to 12 hours.

To make the tomato sauce, put the olive oil in a large saucepan. Set the pan over medium heat. Add the onion and cook, stirring occasionally, until tender and translucent, about 10 minutes. Add the garlic and cook, stirring constantly, for 1 minute longer. Add the tomatoes, tomato paste, and oregano, stirring to combine. Raise the heat to medium-high and cook, stirring occasionally and breaking up the tomatoes with a wooden spoon, until the sauce is thick, 10 to 15 minutes. Taste the sauce (careful, it's hot!) and season with salt and pepper. Let cool and transfer to a bowl.

Position a rack in the lower third of the oven and preheat the oven to 425°F. Lightly sprinkle 2 rimmed baking sheets with cornmeal. (If the dough has risen in the refrigerator, remove the bowl from the refrigerator and let the dough come to room temperature for about 1 hour before continuing.) Turn out the dough onto a floured work surface and, using a knife, divide into 12 equal pieces.

> ### Pizza art
> *Use your favorite toppings to make pretty designs, like flowers, faces, or fun patterns to create a unique piece of food art.*

TOPPING IDEAS

Shredded mozzarella cheese

Sliced mushrooms

Sliced cooked Italian sausage

Sliced pepperoni

Halved cherry tomatoes

Sliced pitted olives

Sliced zucchini

Roasted red bell pepper slices

Cooked broccoli florets

Set out your favorite toppings in separate bowls, along with the tomato sauce, and let the party begin! Give each person a piece of dough. Gently press and stretch the dough into a circle about 7 inches in diameter. (Don't work the dough too much or it won't hold its shape.) Spread the round with a thin layer of tomato sauce, sprinkle with some cheese, and add the toppings of your choice.

Place 2 pizza rounds on each prepared baking sheet and bake one sheet at a time until the crust is golden and the cheese is bubbly, 12 to 15 minutes. Remove the baking sheet from the oven. Repeat to bake the remaining pizza rounds.

Let the pizzas cool for a few minutes on the baking sheet, and then use a wide metal spatula to transfer them to a cutting board. Cut each one into quarters and serve each guest his or her own creation.

Pizza Party Game Plan

Before the party, make the pizza dough, cook the tomato sauce, and divide the dough into 12 portions. Then when guests show up, set out as many different types of toppings as you like, put the tomato sauce in a bowl, and give each person a piece of dough to shape and top. You'll have to bake the pizzas two at a time, but serve them hot out of the oven—and encourage sharing!

Rosemary Roast Chicken

The next time you want to make a really special meal for your family, pull out this recipe! This juicy roasted chicken is great served with Creamiest Mashed Potatoes (page 106) and Sautéed Green Beans with Almonds (page 105).

MAKES 4-6 SERVINGS

Juice of 1 lemon

¼ cup olive oil

3 tablespoons whole-grain Dijon mustard

2 tablespoons chopped fresh rosemary leaves

¼ teaspoon salt

Pinch of ground black pepper

2 bone-in chicken breast halves

2 chicken drumsticks

2 bone-in chicken thighs

In a large glass or ceramic baking dish, stir together the lemon juice, olive oil, mustard, rosemary, salt, and pepper. Add the chicken pieces and use tongs to turn and coat them with the marinade. Cover the baking dish with plastic wrap and refrigerate for at least 1 hour or up to overnight, turning the chicken pieces once.

Remove the baking dish from the refrigerator and uncover. If the chicken pieces are skin side down, turn them skin side up. Let the chicken stand at room temperature for 30 minutes. After 15 minutes, preheat the oven to 400°F.

Put the baking dish in the oven and roast the chicken until the skin is browned, about 50 minutes. Remove the dish from the oven. To test if the chicken is done, slide the tip of a paring knife into and out of the thickest part of a drumstick. The juices should run clear; if they are pink, return the chicken to the oven, cook for 5 to 10 minutes longer, and then test again.

Using tongs, transfer the chicken pieces to a platter. Spoon some of the cooking juices over the top and serve right away.

Fish Tacos with Slaw

In addition to the tangy slaw, you can top these yummy tacos with a squeeze of lime juice, a dollop of sour cream, a sprinkle of fresh chopped cilantro, or spoonfuls of salsa. Or, if you like, add them all!

MAKES 6 SERVINGS

SLAW

4 cups finely shredded green and purple cabbage

3 tablespoons chopped fresh cilantro

¼ cup chopped green onion (optional)

¼ cup fresh lime juice

2 teaspoons sugar

Salt

12 corn tortillas

1 pound skinless, boneless firm white fish fillets, such as cod or snapper

Canola oil for brushing the fish

Ground black pepper

 To make the slaw, in a large bowl, combine the cabbage, cilantro, green onion (if using), lime juice, sugar, and ¼ teaspoon salt and mix well. Let stand at room temperature for 20 minutes, and then taste and add more salt if you like. Cover the bowl with plastic wrap and refrigerate until you're ready to assemble the tacos.

Ask an adult to help you prepare a medium-high fire in a gas or charcoal grill or have ready a stovetop grill pan. Stack the tortillas and wrap them in aluminum foil.

Lightly brush the fish on both sides with canola oil and season with salt and pepper. If using a stovetop grill pan, preheat it over medium-high heat on the stovetop; brush the grill pan with oil. If using the grill, clean and oil the grill grate. Place the fish fillets on the grill grate or grill pan. Cook, turning once with a wide metal spatula, until browned on both sides and the flesh is opaque throughout, 3 to 4 minutes on each side. Meanwhile, place the foil-wrapped tortillas on the grill grate or grill pan and warm them, turning the packet once or twice, for about 5 minutes. Transfer the fish to a plate and divide the fillets into 12 equal pieces, discarding any bones.

Unwrap the tortillas. To assemble each serving, place 2 warm tortillas on a plate, top each one with a piece of fish, and add some slaw. Serve the tacos right away as you assemble each serving.

Baked Chicken Parmesan

Crisp, crunchy chicken topped with tangy tomato sauce and gooey mozzarella cheese is an Italian-American favorite. To make Baked Eggplant Parmesan, a vegetarian version that's every bit as yummy, see the variation at the end of this recipe. *Mangia!*

3 tablespoons olive oil, plus more for greasing the baking dish

6 small boneless, skinless chicken breast halves

Salt

1 cup all-purpose flour

3 large eggs, beaten

1½ cups plain dried bread crumbs

½ cup grated Parmesan cheese

1 pound fresh mozzarella cheese, cut into thin slices

3 cups homemade or store-bought marinara sauce

Pour the olive oil onto a rimmed baking sheet and use a pastry brush to coat the entire surface. Place 1 chicken breast half inside a zipper-lock freezer bag and pound with a meat pounder until it is ½ inch thick. Transfer to a large plate and repeat with the remaining chicken breast halves. Season the chicken breasts on both sides with salt.

Preheat the oven to 400°F. Put the flour, eggs, and bread crumbs in 3 separate shallow bowls or baking dishes. Line up the bowls in that order from left to right. Stir the Parmesan into the bread crumbs.

One at a time, coat the chicken breasts on both sides with flour and tap off the excess. Dip the flour-coated chicken into the eggs, turn to coat, and allow the excess to drip off. Finally, dip the breasts into the bread crumbs and turn to coat both sides, pressing so that the bread crumbs stick. Place on the prepared baking sheet in a single layer.

Bake for 15 minutes. Remove the baking sheet from the oven. Using a wide metal spatula, carefully turn the chicken breasts. Continue to bake until golden on both sides, about 15 minutes longer. Remove the baking sheet from the oven and set aside. Leave the oven on.

> **Italian feast**
> *Serve this yummy cheesy dish with a big pile of buttered spaghetti or sautéed spinach or both!*

Lightly grease a 9-by-13-inch baking dish with olive oil. Pour in 2 cups of marinara sauce and spread it into an even layer. Use a spatula to arrange the warm chicken breasts in the baking dish, overlapping them slightly, and pour the remaining 1 cup of marinara sauce evenly over the top, then lay the mozzarella slices on top. Bake until the cheese is melted and the sauce is bubbling, about 20 minutes.

Remove the baking dish from the oven. Let cool for 10 minutes and serve.

Variation: Eggplant Parmesan

Pour 3 tablespoons of olive oil onto each of 2 rimmed baking sheets and use a pastry brush to coat the entire surfaces. Trim 2 small globe eggplants (1½ pounds total) and slice them into ½-inch-thick rounds. Sprinkle both sides of the slices with salt and set aside for 20 minutes (the salt will help remove some of the bitterness from the eggplant). Pat the slices dry with paper towels. Follow the recipe for Baked Chicken Parmesan, using the eggplant slices in place of the chicken breasts, arranging them in a single layer on the prepared baking sheets. When arranging the baked eggplant in the prepared baking dish, tuck the mozzarella between the eggplant slices instead of placing it on top. Increase the amount of marinara to 4 cups. Bake as directed.

Spaghetti & Meatballs

A mound of spaghetti topped with turkey meatballs and cheese? Yes, please! The meatballs are also delish stuffed into crusty rolls and topped with tomato sauce and Parmesan cheese.

MAKES 4-6 SERVINGS

SAUCE

2 tablespoons olive oil

½ yellow onion, chopped

1 clove garlic, minced

One 15-ounce can tomato purée

One 14½-ounce can diced tomatoes with juices

One 6-ounce can tomato paste

2 tablespoons dried oregano

Salt and ground black pepper

To make the sauce, pour the olive oil into a large saucepan. Set the pan over medium heat. Add the onion and garlic and cook, stirring occasionally, until the onion is soft, about 5 minutes. Add the tomato purée, diced tomatoes and their juices, tomato paste, and oregano and stir to combine. Bring to a simmer, and then reduce the heat to medium-low and cook, stirring occasionally, until thickened, about 20 minutes. Season to taste with salt and pepper. Remove the pan from the heat, cover, and set aside.

~ *Continued on page 87* ~

Super sauce
This yummy spaghetti sauce is loaded with flavor. You can double it and freeze half for later, too!

~ *Continued from page 84* ~

MEATBALLS

2 tablespoons olive oil

1½ pounds ground dark-meat turkey

1 cup fresh bread crumbs

½ cup grated Parmesan cheese

2 large eggs

1 tablespoon dried oregano

Salt and ground black pepper

1 pound spaghetti

Grated Parmesan cheese for serving

To make the meatballs, preheat the oven to 450°F. Pour the olive oil onto a rimmed baking sheet and use a pastry brush to coat the entire surface.

In a large bowl, combine the ground turkey, bread crumbs, Parmesan, eggs, and oregano. Season with salt and pepper. Using clean hands, mix until well combined. Scoop out tablespoon-sized portions of the turkey mixture, rolling each one between your palms to form a small ball.

Place the meatballs in a single layer on the baking sheet, making sure they don't touch. Bake until the meatballs are browned and cooked through, about 15 minutes.

Remove the baking sheet from the oven and transfer the meatballs to the pan of tomato sauce. Set the pan over low heat and cook, stirring occasionally and gently, about 20 minutes.

While the meatballs simmer, fill a large pot three-fourths full of water. Set the pot over high heat and bring the water to a boil. Add 1 tablespoon salt and the spaghetti, stir well, and cook according to the package directions until al dente (tender but firm at the center). Drain the spaghetti in a colander set in the sink and divide among warmed serving bowls. Ladle sauce and meatballs over the top, sprinkle with Parmesan, and serve right away.

Teriyaki Chicken & Veggies

This stir-fry is quick and easy to cook, and the different-colored veggies make it pretty, too. There's lots of sweet-and-salty sauce in this dish, so make sure to serve it with steamed rice for soaking up the yumminess!

MAKES 4 SERVINGS

TERIYAKI SAUCE

⅓ cup low-sodium chicken broth

⅓ cup low-sodium soy sauce

1 tablespoon packed light brown sugar

2 teaspoons cornstarch

1 large clove garlic, smashed

½ red bell pepper

1 tablespoon olive oil

8 baby carrots, cut lengthwise into sticks

1 heaping cup sliced mushrooms

1 cup sugar snap peas or snow peas, trimmed and cut in half

2 boneless, skinless chicken breast halves, cut crosswise into ¼-inch strips

Steamed jasmine rice for serving

To make the sauce, put the chicken broth, soy sauce, brown sugar, cornstarch, and garlic in a food processor. Cover and process until smooth, about 30 seconds.

Using a paring knife, remove the stem, seedy core, and whitish ribs and discard. Cut the pepper lengthwise into thin strips.

Put the olive oil in a large frying pan. Set the pan over medium heat. Heat the oil for 1 minute, and then add the carrots and the bell pepper strips. Stir to coat with oil, cover, and cook, stirring occasionally, until the veggies are crisp-tender, about 5 minutes. Stir in the mushrooms and cook until they're nearly tender, about 3 minutes. Add the sugar snap peas and the chicken and cook, stirring often, until the chicken is no longer pink, about 5 minutes.

Whisk the sauce, then pour it into the pan and cook, stirring constantly, until the sauce is simmering and slightly thickened, 1 to 2 minutes.

Spoon rice onto individual plates, top with the stir-fry and some sauce, and serve right away.

Hawaiian Chicken Kebabs

Food on a stick is so much fun to cook and to eat! With chunks of pineapple, cubes of chicken, and a soy-ginger sauce, these kebabs are loaded with yummy sweet and savory flavors. Serve them with steamed rice and sugar snap peas.

MAKES 6-8 SERVINGS

½ cup pineapple juice

3 tablespoons olive oil, plus more for brushing the kebabs

2 tablespoons soy sauce

2 tablespoons packed light brown sugar

1 tablespoon peeled and grated fresh ginger

1 clove garlic, minced

3 boneless, skinless chicken breast halves (about 1½ pounds total), cut into 1½-inch cubes

2 cups fresh pineapple, cut into 1-inch chunks

Have ready 12 to 16 skewers. (If you're using wooden skewers, soak them in water to cover for at least 15 minutes, and then drain.) Ask an adult to help you prepare a medium fire in a gas or charcoal grill or have ready a stovetop grill pan.

In a small bowl, combine the pineapple juice, olive oil, soy sauce, sugar, ginger, and garlic. Stir until the sugar dissolves. This is the basting sauce.

Thread 2 or 3 chicken pieces alternately with 2 or 3 pineapple chunks onto each skewer. Brush the kebabs lightly with olive oil, and then brush them liberally with some of the basting sauce.

If using a stovetop grill pan, preheat it over medium-high heat on the stovetop; brush the grill pan with oil. If using the grill, clean and oil the grill grate.

Place the kebabs on the grate or grill pan. Cook, brushing them often with basting sauce and turning with tongs as needed, until lightly browned on all sides and the chicken is opaque throughout when cut into with a knife, 7 to 10 minutes. If you have any basting sauce left over, discard it.

Transfer the kebabs to a platter and serve right away.

Ham, Cheese & Roasted Red Pepper Panini

A panini is a sandwich that's pressed during cooking so that the bread becomes nice and crisp and the cheese gets extra gooey. For the ultimate grilled cheese sandwich, skip the roasted pepper and ham and use two or three different types of cheese.

MAKES 2 PANINI

4 slices sourdough bread

8 slices provolone, Monterey jack, or Swiss cheese

1 jarred roasted red pepper, drained and finely chopped

4 slices Black Forest ham or honey ham

2 tablespoons unsalted butter, at room temperature

Lay 2 of the bread slices on a clean work surface and top each with 2 slices of cheese, half of the chopped roasted pepper, 2 slices of ham, and another 2 slices of cheese. Top each sandwich with 1 of the remaining bread slices. Spread the butter on the outside of the sandwiches, dividing it evenly among the sides.

Place a griddle or large nonstick frying pan over medium heat and let it heat for 3 minutes. Put the panini on the griddle and cook, turning once, until golden brown on both sides, 2 to 3 minutes per side. As the panini cook, use a wide metal spatula to gently press them down once or twice on each side.

Using the spatula, transfer the panini to a cutting board. Let cool for 1 to 2 minutes to let the cheese set slightly. Cut each panini in half diagonally. Serve right away.

Sandwich stuffings
Create your favorite panini with toppings you love, like smoked turkey, chopped tomatoes, or a smear of pesto.

Sesame Noodles with Peanut Sauce

Here, noodles are tossed with a rich, peanutty sauce and crisp, colorful veggies. Broccoli florets, sugar snap peas, or chopped asparagus are awesome substitutes for the carrots or snow peas. Or add 2 cups shredded cooked chicken along with the cooked veggies.

MAKES 5 SERVINGS

2 carrots

Salt

¼ pound snow peas, trimmed

½ pound spaghetti, broken in half

1 teaspoon toasted sesame oil

3½ tablespoons fresh lime juice

3 tablespoons soy sauce

2½ tablespoons creamy peanut butter

2 teaspoons well-stirred tahini

1½ teaspoons Asian chile paste, such as sambal oelek (optional)

¼ cup chopped roasted peanuts

 Peel the carrots and slice them diagonally into ⅛-inch-thick ovals. Cut each oval lengthwise into matchsticks.

Fill a large pot three-fourths full of water. Set the pot over high heat and bring the water to a boil. Add 2 teaspoons salt and the snow peas and cook just until the peas are crisp-tender, about 1 minute. Using a slotted spoon, transfer the peas to a medium bowl. Add the carrot matchsticks to the pot and cook until just crisp-tender, about 2 minutes. Transfer to the bowl with snow peas and set aside. Add the spaghetti to the boiling water and cook according to package directions until al dente (tender but still firm at the center). Reserve ¼ cup of the cooking water, and then drain noodles in a colander set in the sink. Return the noodles to the pot, add the sesame oil, and toss with tongs until evenly coated.

In a small bowl, whisk together the lime juice, soy sauce, peanut butter, tahini, chile paste (if using), and reserved pasta water until blended. Add the mixture to the pasta along with the vegetables and toss with tongs until evenly coated and the veggies are evenly distributed.

Transfer the noodles to a serving bowl, sprinkle with the chopped peanuts, and serve right away.

Baked Penne with Spinach & Cheese

This baked pasta is a hearty, super-tasty vegetarian dish.
If you're a meat lover, you won't even notice that it's meat-free!
Cheesy Garlic Bread (page 102) is perfect to serve alongside.

MAKES **6** SERVINGS

1 tablespoon unsalted butter, plus more for greasing the baking dish

Salt

¾ pound penne pasta

One 10-ounce container fresh baby spinach

1 cup crumbled feta cheese

1 cup sour cream

½ cup plain whole-milk yogurt

½ cup shredded mozzarella or grated Parmesan cheese

 Preheat the oven to 375°F. Butter a 9-by-13-inch baking dish.

Fill a large pot three-fourths full of water. Set the pot over high heat and bring the water to a boil. Add 1 tablespoon salt and the pasta, stir well, and cook the pasta according to the package directions until al dente (tender but still firm at the center). Drain in a colander set in the sink, transfer the pasta to a bowl, and set aside. Return the colander to the sink.

Add the butter to a large frying pan. Set the pan over medium heat. When the butter has melted, add the spinach in 2 or 3 batches, stirring until slightly wilted before adding the next batch. Stir in a pinch of salt and cook until the spinach is completely wilted. Drain the spinach in the colander and press down on it with a rubber spatula to remove as much liquid as possible. Transfer the spinach to a cutting board and finely chop.

In a large bowl, stir the feta, sour cream, yogurt, and spinach until well combined. Add the pasta and stir until evenly coated. Pour the mixture into the prepared baking dish, spread into an even layer, and sprinkle the mozzarella evenly over the top. Bake until hot and bubbly, about 30 minutes.

Remove the baking dish from the oven. Serve right away.

Sweet Potato Chips

Did you know you can make potato chips at home in your oven? And it's super easy! This version uses sweet potatoes, but you can use the same method with russet potatoes or try a variety of root vegetables.

MAKES 2 SERVINGS

1 small sweet potato (about ¼ pound), peeled

1 tablespoon olive oil

Salt

 Preheat the oven to 400°F. Line a baking sheet with parchment paper.

Using the thinnest slicing disk on a food processor or a sharp knife and a very steady hand, slice the sweet potato crosswise into very thin ⅛-inch rounds. Put the slices in a large bowl and drizzle with the olive oil. Using your hands, gently toss the slices very gently until evenly coated.

Lay the sweet potato slices in a single layer, overlapping them as little as possible, on the prepared baking sheet. Use a pastry brush to spread the oil remaining in the bowl on any uncoated slices. Bake for 10 minutes. Remove the baking sheet from the oven and, using a wide metal spatula, turn over all of the slices. Sprinkle with ¼ teaspoon salt and continue to bake until the slices are dry and some are lightly browned, about 10 minutes longer. Check often during the last few minutes of baking.

Remove the baking sheet from the oven and slide the chips into a serving bowl. Sprinkle with a little more salt and serve warm.

Cheesy Garlic Bread

Who can resist buttery garlic bread with lots of melted cheese? It's the perfect companion to any soup or pasta dish, and it's also great on its own as a savory after-school or movie-night snack.

MAKES 8 SERVINGS

½ cup unsalted butter

3 large cloves garlic, minced

1 teaspoon minced fresh flat-leaf parsley (optional)

1 loaf Italian bread, cut in half horizontally

1½ cups shredded mozzarella cheese or grated Parmesan cheese

 Preheat the oven to 450°F.

In a small frying pan, combine the butter and garlic. Set the pan over medium heat. Cook, stirring constantly, until the butter is completely melted. Stir in the parsley (if using) and remove the pan from the heat.

Place the bread halves cut sides up on a rimmed baking sheet. Using a pastry brush, brush the butter mixture evenly on the cut sides of the bread. Top with the cheese, dividing it evenly between the halves. Bake until the cheese is melted and the edges are toasted and golden brown, 5 to 7 minutes.

Remove the baking sheet from the oven. Let the bread cool slightly, and then transfer to a cutting board. Cut the bread crosswise into thick slices and serve right away.

Sautéed Green Beans with Almonds

These green beans get all dressed up with a few simple additions: sweet-tart balsamic vinegar, creamy butter, and toasty almonds. This dish is the perfect addition to a special dinner or holiday meal, but it's also easy enough to make on a school night!

MAKES 4-6 SERVINGS

2 tablespoons sliced almonds

Salt

1 pound thin green beans, trimmed and cut into 1-inch lengths

1 tablespoon unsalted butter

2 teaspoons balsamic vinegar

Ground black pepper

Put the almonds in a small frying pan. Set the pan over medium heat. Cook, stirring occasionally, until the almonds are lightly browned and smell toasty, 4 to 5 minutes. Transfer to a bowl and let cool completely.

Fill a large saucepan half full with water. Set the pan over high heat and bring the water to a boil. Add 1 teaspoon salt and the beans and boil until the beans are bright green and just tender, 3 to 5 minutes. Drain the beans in a colander set in the sink and rinse under cold running water. Drain well.

Add the butter to a large frying pan. Set the pan over low heat. When the butter is melted, add the green beans and the vinegar. Raise the heat to medium and cook, tossing with tongs, until the beans are heated through, about 1 minute. Taste the beans (careful, they're hot!) and season with salt and pepper. Transfer to a bowl or platter, sprinkle with the almonds, and serve right away.

Creamiest Mashed Potatoes

Have you ever met anyone who doesn't love a big, pillowy mound of creamy mashed potatoes? For a super-yummy, cheesy twist, stir in ½ cup grated Cheddar or Monterey jack along with the milk mixture.

MAKES 6-8 SERVINGS

Salt

2 pounds Yukon gold potatoes, peeled and quartered

½ cup whole milk

½ cup heavy cream

2 tablespoons unsalted butter, plus 1 tablespoon melted butter

Fill a large saucepan about three-fourths full of water and add 1 tablespoon salt and the potatoes. Set the pan over medium-high heat and bring to a boil. Reduce the heat to medium-low and simmer, uncovered, until you can easily slide a skewer into and out of the potatoes, about 20 minutes. Drain the potatoes in a colander set in the sink.

Transfer the potatoes to a large bowl and mash with a potato masher until very smooth. Cover the bowl with a clean kitchen towel to keep the potatoes warm.

In a small saucepan, combine the milk, cream, and butter. Set the pan over medium heat and bring to a simmer. Gradually add the hot milk mixture to the potatoes while beating with a fork. The potatoes should be smooth and thick. Taste the potatoes, season with salt, and top with the melted butter. Transfer to a bowl and serve right away.

Gold & creamy
Sweet and smooth, Yukon gold potatoes make the best mash, but you can also use russet potatoes in a pinch.

Refried Black Beans

Refried beans are the perfect side to tacos and enchiladas and can be spread onto tostadas or stuffed into burritos. This recipe makes smooth refried beans, but if you like them chunky, purée only two-thirds of the cooked beans.

MAKES 6-8 SERVINGS

1 cup dried black beans

1 small yellow onion, chopped

2 large cloves garlic

1 teaspoon ground cumin

Salt

¼ cup canola oil

½ lime

Cotija cheese or shredded Monterey jack for serving

Pick over the beans, discarding any pebbles and grit. Place the beans in a medium bowl, add water to cover by 4 inches, and soak overnight at room temperature.

Drain the beans in a colander set in the sink, rinse well under running cold water, and transfer to a large saucepan. Add the onion, garlic, cumin, and water to cover by 1 inch. Set the pan over high heat and bring to a gentle boil, using a spoon to skim off any foam that forms on the surface. Reduce the heat to medium-low and simmer for 45 minutes, stirring occasionally. Add 1 teaspoon salt and more water if needed to keep the beans submerged, and continue to cook until the beans are very tender, 15 to 20 minutes longer. Turn off the heat and let the beans cool in their cooking liquid.

Remove about ¼ cup of the cooking liquid, and then drain the beans in a colander set in the sink. Put the beans in a food processor and process until smooth. If the purée is too stiff to move smoothly, add the reserved cooking liquid 1 tablespoon at a time to achieve a very smooth, thick paste.

Put the canola oil in a medium frying pan or sauté pan. Set the pan over medium heat. Add the beans, stir well to incorporate with the oil, and cook, stirring constantly, until the beans sizzle and pull away from the sides of the pan, about 7 minutes. Taste the beans (careful, they're hot!), adjust the seasoning with salt, and squeeze in as much lime juice as you like. Transfer to a bowl, sprinkle with cheese, and serve right away.

Stuffed Baked Potatoes

Potatoes that are baked, hollowed out, stuffed with a cheesy potato mixture, and then baked again make a hearty side dish. You can easily turn them into a meal by adding ¼ cup chopped ham and ¼ cup chopped cooked broccoli florets to the stuffing mixture.

MAKES 4-8 SERVINGS

4 russet baking potatoes, scrubbed

½ cup sour cream

¼ cup whole milk

1¼ cups shredded Cheddar cheese

Salt and ground black pepper

 Preheat the oven to 375°F.

Poke the potatoes all over with the tip of a paring knife. Put the potatoes in the oven, directly on the oven rack, and bake until you can easily pierce them with a skewer or dinner fork, about 1 hour.

Remove the potatoes from the oven, but leave the oven on. Set the potatoes aside until they are cool enough to handle.

Cut the potatoes in half lengthwise (careful, the insides may still be hot!). Using a spoon, scoop the potato flesh into a mixing bowl, being careful not to poke through the skin on the bottom and sides. Try to leave a wall of potato flesh about ¼ inch thick, so that the skin won't break when you stuff it. Set the skins, cut sides up, in a baking dish just large enough to hold them in a single layer. Add the sour cream and milk to the potato flesh. Using the spoon, stir and mash the mixture until smooth, and then stir in half of the cheese. Taste and season with salt and pepper.

Using the spoon, scoop the potato mixture into the potato skins, dividing it evenly. Sprinkle with the remaining cheese, dividing it evenly. Bake until the cheese is melted and the potatoes are heated through, about 15 minutes.

Remove the baking dish from the oven and serve right away.

Buttery Peas with Mint

Take simple frozen peas and mix them with butter and mint and you'll experience a taste explosion! This super-easy side dish is great alongside roasted chicken, grilled fish, or a seared steak.

MAKES 4-6 SERVINGS

2 cups frozen peas

1 tablespoon chopped fresh mint leaves

1 tablespoon unsalted butter, cut into pieces

Salt

Put about ½ inch of water in a medium saucepan, add the peas, and cover. Set the pan over high heat and bring to a boil. Reduce the heat to medium and simmer until the peas are just tender, 4 to 5 minutes.

Pour the peas into a colander set in the sink. Drain well—shaking the colander helps—and return the peas to the saucepan over medium heat. Add the mint, butter, and several pinches of salt and stir until the butter melts. Transfer to a bowl and serve right away.

Roasted Carrots

Sweet roasted carrots are a terrific accompaniment to almost any main course—that is, if you don't eat all of them before they make it to the table! Try to find multicolored carrots, sold in bunches, for a fun, festive-looking side dish.

MAKES 4 SERVINGS

1 pound carrots, trimmed

1 tablespoon unsalted butter, cut into little pieces

2 tablespoons brown sugar

¼ teaspoon ground ginger

½ teaspoon salt

Ground black pepper

 Preheat the oven to 400°F.

Peel the carrots and cut them crosswise into thirds. Cut each piece in half lengthwise, and then cut any extra-thick pieces in half lengthwise again, forming wedges. Place the carrots in an even layer on a rimmed baking sheet and dot with the butter.

Roast the carrots, stirring occasionally, until tender and beginning to brown, about 30 minutes.

While the carrots are roasting, in a small bowl, stir together the brown sugar, ginger, and salt.

Remove the baking sheet from the oven. Sprinkle the carrots evenly with the sugar mixture. Return the baking sheet to the oven and continue to roast the carrots until the sugar is melted and syrupy, about 5 minutes.

Remove the baking sheet from the oven and transfer the carrots to a platter or bowl. Season with pepper. Serve right away.

Roasted veggies
Swap out the cauliflower for asparagus spears or broccoli florets and roast in the same way.

Roasted Cauliflower

Roasting vegetables in a hot oven caramelizes their natural sugars and brings out a rich, nutty sweetness. If you like, substitute chopped cooked bacon, chopped olives, or currants for the lemon zest that's tossed in just before serving.

MAKES 6-8 SERVINGS

1 head cauliflower (about 1½ pounds)
3 tablespoons olive oil
½ teaspoon salt
Grated zest of 1 lemon

 Preheat the oven to 425°F.

Trim off and discard the green outer leaves, and then cut the cauliflower from top to bottom into quarters. Cut out the core from each quarter, and then cut the cauliflower into medium florets.

Arrange the cauliflower in a single layer on a rimmed baking sheet and drizzle with the olive oil. Sprinkle with the salt and toss until the florets are evenly coated with oil.

Roast the cauliflower until golden on the bottom, about 15 minutes. Remove the baking sheet from the oven and use a wide metal spatula to turn over the florets. Continue to roast until tender and golden on the second sides, 10 to 15 minutes longer.

Remove the baking sheet from the oven and transfer the cauliflower to a platter. Sprinkle with the lemon zest, toss to combine, and serve right away.

Index

A

Almonds
    Fruit & Granola Bars, 34
    Sautéed Green Beans
        with Almonds, 105
Avocados
    BLT Salad with Avocado, 45
    Chopped Green Salad, 47
    Guacamole & Star Chips, 26
    Taco Salad, 39
    Turkey Club Sandwiches, 65

B

Bacon
    BLT Salad with Avocado, 45
    Turkey Club Sandwiches, 65
Baked Chicken Parmesan, 80
Baked Penne with Spinach
    & Cheese, 96
Bars, Fruit & Granola, 34
Beans
    Lemony Hummus, 32
    Refried Black Beans, 109
    Taco Salad, 39
    Turkey Chili, 53
Beef
    Spiced Beef Tacos, 66
    Taco Salad, 39
Breads
    Cheese Toasts, 54
    Cheesy Garlic Bread, 102
Buttery Peas with Mint, 115

C

Caprese Kebabs, 22
Carrots
    Roasted Carrots, 116
    Sesame Noodles with
        Peanut Sauce, 95
    Teriyaki Chicken & Veggies, 88
Cauliflower, Roasted, 119
Cheese
    Baked Chicken Parmesan, 80
    Baked Penne with Spinach
        & Cheese, 96
    Caprese Kebabs, 22
    Cheese Toasts, 54
    Cheesy Garlic Bread, 102
    Creamy Tomato Soup with
        Cheese Toasts, 54
    Eggplant Parmesan, 81
    Ham, Cheese & Roasted
        Red Pepper Panini, 92
    Homemade Pizza, 70
    Hot Cheese Dip, 33
    Spiced Beef Tacos, 66
    Stuffed Baked Potatoes, 112
    Sweet-n-Salty Popcorn, 19
    Taco Salad, 39
    Turkey Sliders with Aioli, 61
Chicken
    Baked Chicken Parmesan, 80
    Chicken Noodle Soup, 48
    Chinese Chicken Salad, 46
    Greek Salad Pitas, 40
    Hawaiian Chicken Kebabs, 91
    Rosemary Roast Chicken, 75
    Teriyaki Chicken & Veggies, 88

Chili, Turkey, 53
Chinese Chicken Salad, 46
Chopped Green Salad, 47
Chowder, Corn & Potato, 51
Cooking tools, 12
Cooking tips
    handling hot equipment, 11
    handling sharp tools, 11
    help from adults, 8, 11
    staying organized, 11
Corn
    Corn & Potato Chowder, 51
    Griddled Corn Fritters
        with Lime, 31
Creamiest Mashed Potatoes, 106
Creamy Tomato Soup with
    Cheese Toasts, 54
Cucumbers
    Chinese Chicken Salad, 46
    Chopped Green Salad, 47
    Greek Salad Pitas, 40

D

Deviled Eggs, 25
Dips
    Guacamole & Star Chips, 26
    Hot Cheese Dip, 33
    Lemony Hummus, 32

E

Eggplant Parmesan, 81
Eggs, Deviled, 25

F

Fish
    Fish Sticks & Homemade
        Tartar Sauce, 62
    Fish Tacos with Slaw, 76
Fritters, Griddled Corn,
    with Lime, 31
Fruit. *See also specific fruits*
    Fruit & Granola Bars, 34

G

Garlic Bread, Cheesy, 102
Granola, Fruit &, Bars, 34
Greek Salad Pitas, 40
Green Beans, Sautéed,
    with Almonds, 105
Griddled Corn Fritters
    with Lime, 31
Guacamole & Star Chips, 26

H

Ham, Cheese & Roasted Red
    Pepper Panini, 92
Hawaiian Chicken Kebabs, 91
Homemade Pizza, 70
Hot Cheese Dip, 33
Hummus, Lemony, 32

K

Kitchen tools, 13

L

Lemony Hummus, 32
Lettuce
    BLT Salad with Avocado, 45
    Chinese Chicken Salad, 46
    Chopped Green Salad, 47
    Greek Salad Pitas, 40
    Spiced Beef Tacos, 66
    Taco Salad, 39

M

Main dishes
    Baked Chicken Parmesan, 80
    Baked Penne with Spinach
        & Cheese, 96
    Eggplant Parmesan, 81
    Fish Sticks & Homemade
        Tartar Sauce, 62
    Fish Tacos with Slaw, 76
    Ham, Cheese & Roasted Red
        Pepper Panini, 92
    Hawaiian Chicken Kebabs, 91
    Homemade Pizza, 70
    Rosemary Roast Chicken, 75
    Sesame Noodles with
        Peanut Sauce, 95
    Spaghetti & Meatballs, 84
    Spiced Beef Tacos, 66
    Teriyaki Chicken & Veggies, 88
    Turkey Club Sandwiches, 65
    Turkey Sliders with Aioli, 61
Meat. *See* Bacon; Beef; Ham

N

Noodles
    Chicken Noodle Soup, 48
    Sesame Noodles with
        Peanut Sauce, 95
Nuts
    Fruit & Granola Bars, 34
    Sautéed Green Beans with
        Almonds, 105
    Sesame Noodles with
        Peanut Sauce, 95

O

Oats
    Fruit & Granola Bars, 34

P

Pasta
    Baked Penne with Spinach
        & Cheese, 96
    Spaghetti & Meatballs, 84
Peanut Sauce, Sesame Noodles
    with, 95
Peas
    Buttery Peas with Mint, 115
    Chinese Chicken Salad, 46
    Sesame Noodles with
        Peanut Sauce, 95
    Teriyaki Chicken & Veggies, 88
Peppers
    Ham, Cheese & Roasted Red
        Pepper Panini, 92
    Teriyaki Chicken & Veggies, 88

Pineapple
    Hawaiian Chicken Kebabs, 91
Pizza, Homemade, 70
Popcorn, Sweet-n-Salty, 19
Pork. See Bacon; Ham
Potatoes
    Corn & Potato Chowder, 51
    Creamiest Mashed Potatoes, 106
    Stuffed Baked Potatoes, 112
    Sweet Potato Chips, 101
Poultry. See Chicken; Turkey

R

Refried Black Beans, 109
Roasted Carrots, 116
Roasted Cauliflower, 119
Rosemary Roast Chicken, 75

S

Salads
    BLT Salad with Avocado, 45
    Chinese Chicken Salad, 46
    Chopped Green Salad, 47
    Greek Salad Pitas, 40
    Taco Salad, 39
Sandwiches
    Greek Salad Pitas, 40
    Ham, Cheese & Roasted Red
        Pepper Panini, 92
    Turkey Club Sandwiches, 65
    Turkey Sliders with Aioli, 61
Sauces
    Aioli, 61
    Homemade Tartar Sauce, 62
    Peanut Sauce, 95
    Tomato Sauce, 70

Sautéed Green Beans with
    Almonds, 105
Sesame Noodles with
    Peanut Sauce, 95
Side dishes
    Buttery Peas with Mint, 115
    Cheesy Garlic Bread, 102
    Creamiest Mashed Potatoes, 106
    Refried Black Beans, 109
    Roasted Carrots, 116
    Roasted Cauliflower, 119
    Sautéed Green Beans
        with Almonds, 105
    Stuffed Baked Potatoes, 112
    Sweet Potato Chips, 101
Sliders, Turkey, with Aioli, 61
Snacks
    Caprese Kebabs, 22
    Deviled Eggs, 25
    Fruit & Granola Bars, 34
    Griddled Corn Fritters
        with Lime, 31
    Guacamole & Star Chips, 26
    Hot Cheese Dip, 33
    Lemony Hummus, 32
    Sweet-n-Salty Popcorn, 19
Soups
    Chicken Noodle Soup, 48
    Corn & Potato Chowder, 51
    Creamy Tomato Soup with
        Cheese Toasts, 54
    Turkey Chili, 53
Spaghetti & Meatballs, 84
Spiced Beef Tacos, 66
Spinach & Cheese, Baked Penne
    with, 96
Stuffed Baked Potatoes, 112
Sweet-n-Salty Popcorn, 19
Sweet Potato Chips, 101

T

Tacos
    Fish Tacos with Slaw, 76
    Spiced Beef Tacos, 66
Taco Salad, 39
Tartar Sauce, Homemade, 62
Teriyaki Chicken & Veggies, 88
Tomatoes
    BLT Salad with Avocado, 45
    Caprese Kebabs, 22
    Creamy Tomato Soup with
        Cheese Toasts, 54
    Spaghetti & Meatballs, 84
    Spiced Beef Tacos, 66
    Tomato Sauce, 70
    Turkey Club Sandwiches, 65
    Turkey Sliders with Aioli, 61
Tortillas
    Fish Tacos with Slaw, 76
    Guacamole & Star Chips, 26
    Spiced Beef Tacos, 66
    Taco Salad, 39
Turkey
    Spaghetti & Meatballs, 84
    Turkey Chili, 53
    Turkey Club Sandwiches, 65
    Turkey Sliders with Aioli, 61

V

Vegetables. *See also* Side dishes;
    specific vegetables
    Teriyaki Chicken & Veggies, 88

weldonowen

1150 Brickyard Cove Road, Richmond, CA 94801
www.weldonowen.com

WELDON OWEN INTERNATIONAL

President & Publisher Roger Shaw
VP, Sales & Marketing Amy Kaneko
Associate Publisher Amy Marr
Project Editor Kim Laidlaw
Associate Editor Emma Rudolph
Creative Director Kelly Booth
Associate Art Director Lisa Berman
Original Design Alexandra Zeigler
Senior Production Designer Rachel Lopez Metzger
Production Director Chris Hemesath
Associate Production Director Michelle Duggan
Director of Enterprise Systems Shawn Macey
Imaging Manager Don Hill
Photographer Nicole Hill Gerulat
Food Stylist Marian Cooper Cairns
Prop Stylist Veronica Olson
Hair & Makeup Kathy Hill

AMERICAN GIRL COOKING

Conceived and produced by Weldon Owen International
In collaboration with Williams Sonoma, Inc.
3250 Van Ness Avenue, San Francisco, CA 94109

Copyright © 2016 Weldon Owen International,
Williams Sonoma, Inc., and American Girl
All rights reserved, including the right of reproduction in whole or in part in any form.

All American Girl marks are owned by and used under license from American Girl.

Library of Congress Cataloging in Publication data is available

ISBN: 978-1-68188-650-3

10 9 8 7 6 5 4 3 2 1
2024 2023 2022 2021 2020

Printed in China

ACKNOWLEDGMENTS

Weldon Owen wishes to thank the following people for their generous support to help produce this book: David Bornfriend, Pranavi Chopra, Nina & Dan Fife, Shauna Green, Jessica Howell, Christine Lee, Kristene Loayza, Rachel Markowitz, Hristina Misafiris, Jacob Muai, Taylor Olson, Elizabeth Parson, Heather Siembieda, Abby Stolfo, and Dawn Yanagihara

A VERY SPECIAL THANK YOU TO:

Our models: Kailee Bauer, Aeslin Cameron, Georgia Faith, Nathaniel Floyd, Jaden Fode, Hadley Hayes, Ruby Nash, Jasmyn Ramos, Ariela Salas, Sadhana Som

Our locations: The Goodmans, The Parkers, The Swaners
Our party resources: Julie Bluét, Rice by Rice, Shop Sweet Lulu, The Sugar Diva, Tea Collection
Our clothing resources: Rachel Riley (rachelriley.com) and Tea Collection (teacollection.com)

Photography **Nicole Hill Gerulat**

weldon**owen**

Contents

BAKE LIKE YOU MEAN IT! 7

Cookies

19
Thumbprint Cookies

20
Chocolate Whoopie Pies

23
Pinwheel Icebox Cookies

25
Snickerdoodles

26
Elephant Ears

29
Lemony Cookie Flower Pops

33
Chocolate Chip Cookie Sandwiches

34
Zesty Lime Cookies

37
Chewy Coconut Macaroons

38
Sugar Cookies

42 Chocolate Crinkle Cookies

44 Ice Cream Sandwiches

Madeleines

51 Orange Madeleines

52 Chocolate-Dipped Vanilla Madeleines

57 Honey Madeleines

58 Chocolate Madeleines

Cupcakes

63 Pumpkin Cupcakes

64 Devil's Food Cupcakes

69 White Chocolate & Raspberry Cupcakes

70 Sweet Lemony Cupcakes

73 Red Velvet Cupcakes

74 Strawberry Cheesecake Cupcakes

76 Carrot Cupcakes with Cream Cheese Frosting

77 PB & J Cupcakes

79 S'mores Cupcakes

80 Black Bottom Cupcakes

83 Snowball Cupcakes

More Treats

89 Chocolate-Peanut Butter Brownies

90 Strawberry Shortcakes

95 Rocky Road Fudge

96 Banana-Chocolate Chip Bread

99 Caramel-Glazed Blondies

100 Blueberry Turnovers

105 Lemony Berry Bars

106 Chocolate Truffles

109 Raspberry-Chocolate Tartlets

111 Easy Cheesecake Pie

112 Apple Oven Pancake

115 Cherry Crisp

116 Golden Layer Cake with Chocolate Frosting

INDEX **122**

Bake Like You Mean It!

It's easy to understand why baking is so much fun. There's nothing quite as satisfying as measuring and mixing ingredients, putting dough or batter into a hot oven, watching—and smelling!—the transformation during baking, and finally removing delicious sweets from the oven. But the best part is sharing the treats you made with your friends and family.

Whether you follow a recipe step-by-step or add your own unique pizzazz, when you bake with happiness, the results will always be terrific. Perhaps you're the type of baker who sneaks a secret ingredient into the batter, like an extra dash of vanilla extract or a swirl of peanut butter. Or maybe you try to follow a recipe exactly as it is written, so the results are always familiar and yummy. Or do you add your personal touch with bright purple frosting and a scattering of rainbow sprinkles? Whatever your style—whether you're daring, playful, colorful, or classic—baking is a great opportunity to let your personality shine and to create mouthwatering goodies with your own special flair.

Yummy recipes ahead!

In these pages, you'll learn the yummiest baking recipes, from cupcakes to madeleines (little shell-shaped French cakes), cookies to brownies, and a whole lot more. Try Strawberry Cheesecake Cupcakes (page 74) for your next birthday party. Chocolate Madeleines (page 58) are perfect for a tea party, and will impress all of your friends—plus they are super easy to make! Pack a slice or two of Banana–Chocolate Chip Bread (page 96) for your next outdoor adventure, or bake a Golden Layer Cake with Chocolate Frosting (page 116) for your friends or family, just because. Turn the pages to discover the most scrumptious recipes, for any occasion, that will delight any sweet tooth.

Baking with care

Baking is the perfect activity to do with friends and family. Since there are a lot of hot surfaces and sharp objects in the kitchen, always have an adult assist you while baking.

When you see this symbol in the book, it means that you need an adult to help you with all or part of the recipe. Ask for help before continuing.

Tip top baking tips

BE OVEN SMART
Be extra careful when working around a hot oven and hot baking dishes. Always use oven mitts and have an adult help you with taking pans in and out of the oven.

GET HELP WITH APPLIANCES
Electric mixers make mixing batters quick and easy. Always have an adult assist you when using appliances.

STAY ORGANIZED
Staying organized and paying attention are important baking skills. Before you preheat the oven, it's important to read the full recipe and ingredient list. Then it's time to clear a clean surface and lay out all your baking tools and ingredients. Once the food is in the oven, don't forget to set a timer!

The tools you'll need

The recipes in this book use a few basic baking tools. There's no need to go out and buy everything all at once—you can collect tools slowly over time, as you try more and more baking recipes.

★ **Aprons** are handy to help keep your clothes tidy when you are baking.

★ **Cookie cutters** come in all shapes. All-time favorites are butterflies, stars, flowers, and hearts, but use any shape you like.

★ **Cookie sheets**, especially thick, heavy ones, help cookies bake evenly and won't warp in the oven.

★ **Small metal icing spatulas** are good for spreading frosting on cupcakes and cakes. A piping bag fitted with a pastry tip is another way to add frosting or to write fun messages on top of cookies, cakes, and cupcakes.

★ **An electric mixer** makes quick work of batters and frostings, beating egg whites and cream, and more. Always ask an adult for help when using appliances. Use a mixing bowl and wooden spoon or whisk in a pinch.

★ **Madeleine pans** are charming French molds used to create dainty, shell-shaped cakes in a variety of flavors.

★ **Measuring cups and spoons** help you measure your ingredients accurately and easily. Choose graduated sets for dry ingredients and a liquid pitcher for wet ingredients.

★ **Oven mitts or pads** protect your hands from hot pans, oven racks, cookie sheets, and baking dishes. Always ask an adult to help when working near a hot oven or stove.

★ **Parchment paper** is paper that's been treated to give it a nonstick surface. It's used to line cookie sheets and baking pans so that baked goods won't stick. If you don't have parchment paper, you can butter the pans and dust them with flour.

★ **A rubber spatula** is helpful for mixing batters and scraping them into pans, like when you transfer the last bits of batter from a bowl to a muffin pan.

★ **Standard muffin pans,** with 12 cups, are used for the cupcake recipes in this book; for some recipes, you'll need two muffin pans.

Imagination and a good dose of creativity are the two most important baker's tools of all. Have fun!

Kissed by chocolate
Instead of using jam, place a chocolate tear-shaped drop into each cookie indent before baking.

MAKES ABOUT 24 COOKIES

Thumbprint Cookies

Use your thumb to create a small indent in the center of these buttery, almond-scented cookies before baking, and fill each one with your favorite fruity, jewel-toned jams, like raspberry, blackberry, or apricot.

2 cups all-purpose flour

½ teaspoon baking powder

¼ teaspoon salt

1 cup (2 sticks) unsalted butter, at room temperature

½ cup sugar

1 teaspoon finely grated orange zest

¾ teaspoon vanilla extract

¼ teaspoon almond extract

½ cup raspberry, apricot, or blackberry jam

 Position 2 racks in the oven so that they are evenly spaced and preheat the oven to 350°F. Line 2 cookie sheets with parchment paper.

In a medium bowl, whisk together the flour, baking powder, and salt. In a large bowl, using an electric mixer, beat the butter and sugar on medium speed until fluffy and pale, about 3 minutes. Add the orange zest, vanilla, and almond extract and beat on medium speed until combined. Turn off the mixer and scrape down the bowl with a rubber spatula. Add half of the flour mixture and mix on low speed just until blended. Add the rest of the flour mixture and mix just until blended. Scrape down the bowl.

Scoop up a rounded tablespoonful of dough, then use your finger to push the dough onto 1 of the prepared cookie sheets. Fill both cookie sheets with dough, spacing the mounds 2 inches apart. You should be able to fit 12 cookies on each cookie sheet.

Dip your thumb in a little flour and use it to make a dent in each ball of dough. Spoon a small amount of jam into each dent. You can vary the types of jam you use to make different flavors of cookies.

Bake the cookies until lightly browned, about 18 minutes. Ask an adult to help you remove the cookie sheets from the oven and set them on wire racks. Let cool for 10 minutes, then use a metal spatula to move the cookies directly to the racks. Let the cookies cool completely and serve.

MAKES 10 WHOOPIE PIES

Chocolate Whoopie Pies

Is it a pie? Is it a cookie? Is it a cake? You won't even care once you take a bite of these awesome choco-licious treats! And who can resist a sweet, gooey marshmallow filling?

COOKIES

6 tablespoons (¾ stick) unsalted butter, at room temperature

½ cup firmly packed light brown sugar

1 large egg

1 teaspoon vanilla extract

¾ cup all-purpose flour

½ cup unsweetened cocoa powder, sifted

½ teaspoon baking soda

⅛ teaspoon salt

FILLING

1 cup marshmallow creme

½ cup powdered sugar, sifted

4 tablespoons (½ stick) unsalted butter, at room temperature

½ teaspoon vanilla extract

 To make the cookies, in a bowl, using an electric mixer, beat the butter and sugar on medium speed until blended, about 1 minute. Add the egg and vanilla and beat until combined. Turn off the mixer and scrape down the bowl with a rubber spatula. Sift the flour, cocoa, baking soda, and salt into a separate bowl, then add to the butter mixture. Mix on low speed just until blended. Cover the bowl with plastic wrap and refrigerate until the dough is firm, about 2 hours.

Position 2 racks in the oven so that they are evenly spaced and preheat the oven to 350°F. Line 2 cookie sheets with parchment paper.

Moisten your hands with water, scoop up a tablespoonful of the dough, and roll the dough between your palms into a ball. Place the ball on a prepared cookie sheet. Repeat with the rest of the dough, evenly spacing the balls on the cookie sheets and flattening them a little. You should have 20 balls.

Bake the cookies until puffed and slightly firm, 8 to 10 minutes, rotating the pans halfway through (ask an adult for help!). Let the cookies cool for 5 minutes, then use a metal spatula to move them directly to wire racks. Let cool.

To make the filling, in a bowl, using an electric mixer, beat the marshmallow creme, powdered sugar, butter, and vanilla on medium speed until smooth.

Turn half of the cookies bottom side up. Use an icing spatula to spread a dollop of the filling on the surface of each upside-down cookie. Top each with a second cookie, placing the flat side onto the filling. Serve right away.

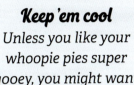

Keep 'em cool
Unless you like your whoopie pies super gooey, you might want to store them in the fridge.

MAKES ABOUT 48 COOKIES

Pinwheel Icebox Cookies

These whimsical cookies are chilled in the refrigerator to help them set into perfect colorful pinwheels. You can make them into cookie pops by inserting ice-pop sticks before baking (follow the directions on page 29).

2 cups all-purpose flour

1 teaspoon baking powder

¼ teaspoon salt

12 tablespoons (1½ sticks) unsalted butter, at room temperature

¾ cup granulated sugar

1 large egg yolk

1½ teaspoons vanilla extract

½ teaspoon red, blue, or green food coloring, plus more as needed

½ teaspoon peppermint extract (optional)

About ½ cup coarse decorating sugar, for rolling (optional)

 In a medium bowl, whisk together the flour, baking powder, and salt. In a large bowl, using an electric mixer, beat the butter and granulated sugar on medium speed until fluffy and pale, about 5 minutes. Turn off the mixer and scrape down the bowl with a rubber spatula. Add the egg yolk and vanilla and beat until combined. Add half of the flour mixture and mix on low speed just until blended. Add the rest of the flour mixture and mix just until blended. Scrape down the bowl.

Dump the dough onto a clean work surface and divide it in half. Add one half back to the bowl and sprinkle the food coloring and peppermint extract, if using, over the dough in the bowl, then gently knead until well combined and evenly colored. If the color is not as dark as you'd like, add more food coloring and gently knead it in.

Cut 4 sheets of wax paper, each one about 18 inches long. Set each dough half on the center of a wax paper sheet and use your hands to shape the dough into a rectangle. Cover each piece of dough with a second wax paper sheet and, one at a time, using a rolling pin, roll out the dough halves into 16-by-10-inch rectangles. Remove the wax paper from one side of each dough rectangle and place the colored rectangle over the plain one. Starting from a long side and using the wax paper on the bottom piece of the dough to help, tightly roll the dough into a log. If you like, scatter the coarse sugar on

~ Continued on page 24 ~

Colorful swirls

Make these cookies even more swirl-erific by coloring both halves of the dough with your favorite colors.

~ *Continued from page 23* ~

a rimmed cookie sheet and roll the log in the sugar to coat the outside. Wrap the log tightly in plastic wrap and refrigerate until firm, at least 1 hour or up to overnight.

Preheat the oven to 350°F. Line 2 cookie sheets with parchment paper. Unwrap the dough log and set it on a cutting board. Ask an adult to help you use a knife to trim off the ends, then cut the log crosswise into ¼-inch-thick slices. Place the slices on the prepared cookie sheets, spacing them about 2 inches apart.

When both cookie sheets are full, bake only 1 cookie sheet at a time until the cookies are firm to the touch (ask an adult for help!), about 12 minutes. Ask an adult to help you remove the cookie sheet from the oven and set it on a wire rack. Let cool for 5 minutes, then use a metal spatula to move the cookies directly to the rack. While the cookies are cooling, put the second cookie sheet in the oven and bake in the same way. After you have removed the cookies from the first cookie sheet, line the empty cookie sheet with new parchment paper and bake the rest of the cookies in the same way. Let the cookies cool completely and serve.

MAKES 36 COOKIES

Snickerdoodles

Toss a ball of sugar cookie dough in cinnamon and sugar before baking, and voilà, you get a snickerdoodle! Not only do they have a super-funny name, these cookies smell amazing while they bake and taste yummy-licious.

2¾ cups all-purpose flour

1 teaspoon baking powder

¼ teaspoon salt

1 cup (2 sticks) unsalted butter, at room temperature

1¾ cups sugar

2 large eggs

2 teaspoons vanilla extract

1 teaspoon ground cinnamon

 Preheat the oven to 350°F. Line 2 cookie sheets with parchment paper.

In a medium bowl, whisk together the flour, baking powder, and salt. In a large bowl, using an electric mixer, beat the butter and 1½ cups of the sugar on medium speed until well blended, about 1 minute. Add the eggs and vanilla and beat on low speed until combined. Turn off the mixer and scrape down the bowl with a rubber spatula. Add the flour mixture and mix just until blended.

In a small bowl, stir together the remaining ¼ cup sugar and the cinnamon. Scoop up a rounded tablespoonful of dough. Scrape the dough off the spoon into the palm of your hand and roll the dough into a ball. Drop the ball in the cinnamon sugar and roll it around to coat it completely. Place the ball on a prepared cookie sheet. Continue scooping, shaping, and rolling the dough in sugar, spacing the balls about 3 inches apart on the cookie sheets. You should be able to fit 12 cookies on each cookie sheet.

When both cookie sheets are full, bake 1 cookie sheet at a time until the edges of the cookies are lightly browned but the tops are barely colored, 10 to 12 minutes. Ask an adult to help you remove the cookie sheet from the oven and set it on a wire rack. Let cool for 5 minutes, then use a metal spatula to move the cookies directly to the rack. While the cookies are cooling, put the second cookie sheet in the oven and bake in the same way. Repeat to bake the rest of the cookies. Let the cookies cool completely and serve.

MAKES ABOUT 20 COOKIES

Elephant Ears

These swirly cookies are made from puff pastry and become sugary-crisp when baked. They're shaped like puffy elephant ears, which is how these treats get their name.

2 tablespoons unsalted butter, melted

½ teaspoon vanilla extract

½ cup granulated sugar

½ cup powdered sugar, sifted

1 sheet frozen puff pastry, thawed

Preheat the oven to 375°F. Line 2 cookie sheets with parchment paper. In a small bowl, stir together the melted butter and vanilla; set aside to cool. In another bowl, using a fork, stir together the granulated and powdered sugars. Measure out ½ cup of the sugar mixture and set aside.

Sprinkle 3 tablespoons of the remaining sugar mixture onto a work surface. Place the puff pastry on top of the sugared surface. Sprinkle more of the sugar mixture on top of the pastry, spreading it evenly with your hands.

Using a rolling pin and beginning at the center of the pastry, roll the pastry into a 10-by-20-inch rectangle, sprinkling a little more sugar mixture underneath and on top of the pastry so the pastry doesn't stick.

Using a pastry brush, brush the butter mixture over the surface of the pastry. Sprinkle evenly with the reserved ½ cup sugar mixture. Starting at one short end, fold a 2-inch-wide band of the pastry over onto itself. Repeat this folding until you reach the center of the pastry (probably 3 folds). Now fold the other end of the rectangle in the same way. Fold one band on top of the other to form a long rectangle. Press to stick it together, then ask an adult to help you cut the rectangle crosswise into ½-inch-thick slices. Place the slices on the prepared cookie sheets, spacing them 2 inches apart.

Bake the pastries 1 cookie sheet at a time until golden, about 15 minutes. Let the cookies cool for 5 minutes, then use a metal spatula to move them directly to a wire rack. Let cool completely and serve.

MAKES ABOUT 12 COOKIE POPS

Lemony Cookie Flower Pops

These adorable cookie pops make awesome gifts for your friends or are super sweet to bring to a bake sale. After the cookies are baked, decorate them to look like your favorite flowers, then show off your cookie bouquet.

COOKIES

2⅓ cups all-purpose flour

¼ teaspoon baking powder

⅛ teaspoon salt

1 cup (2 sticks) unsalted butter, at room temperature

⅔ cup granulated sugar

1 large egg

1½ teaspoons vanilla extract

LEMON ICING

1 cup powdered sugar, sifted

1 tablespoon plus 1 teaspoon lemon juice

2 or 3 drops of food coloring in your favorite color(s)

Sprinkles and/or candies for decorating

 To make the cookies, in a bowl, whisk together the flour, baking powder, and salt. In a large bowl, using an electric mixer, beat the butter and sugar on medium speed until fluffy and pale, about 5 minutes. Turn off the mixer and scrape down the bowl with a rubber spatula. Add the egg and vanilla and beat until well combined. Add the flour mixture and mix just until blended. Scrape down the bowl. Divide the dough in half and press each piece into a disk. Wrap each disk in plastic wrap and refrigerate until firm, at least 1 hour.

Preheat the oven to 350°F. Line 2 cookie sheets with parchment paper. Sprinkle a work surface with flour. Unwrap 1 chilled dough disk and place it on the floured surface. Using a floured rolling pin, roll out the dough disk into a ¼-inch-thick round. With flower-shaped cookie cutters, cut out as many cookies as possible. Use a metal spatula to transfer the cookies to the prepared cookie sheet, spacing them apart. Press the dough scraps into a disk, wrap in plastic wrap, and refrigerate until firm. Repeat with the second chilled dough disk and the scraps. Insert a wooden ice-pop stick into each cookie flower. Bake the cookies 1 cookie sheet at a time until golden, 15 to 20 minutes. Let the cookies cool for 10 minutes, then use a metal spatula to move them directly to a wire rack. Let cool completely.

To make the icing, in a bowl, whisk together the powdered sugar, lemon juice, and food coloring until smooth. Spread the icing onto the cooled cookies with an icing spatula or use a piping bag to decorate with icing, then decorate with sprinkles while the icing is still wet. Let the icing dry, then serve.

MAKES ABOUT 28 SANDWICH COOKIES

Chocolate Chip Cookie Sandwiches

One of the most scrumptious cookies just got even more irresistible! Take two chocolate chip cookies, put a thick layer of super-chocolaty frosting between them, and you've got a new favorite treat. Don't forget a big glass of cold milk!

2 cups all-purpose flour

1 teaspoon baking soda

½ teaspoon salt

1 cup (2 sticks) unsalted butter, at room temperature

¾ cup firmly packed light brown sugar

¾ cup granulated sugar

2 large eggs

2 teaspoons vanilla extract

2 cups semisweet chocolate chips

Chocolate Frosting (page 64)

 Preheat the oven to 350°F. Line 2 cookie sheets with parchment paper.

In a medium bowl, whisk together the flour, baking soda, and salt. In a large bowl, using an electric mixer, beat the butter, brown sugar, and granulated sugar on medium speed until well blended, about 1 minute. Add the eggs and vanilla and beat on low speed until well combined. Turn off the mixer and scrape down the bowl with a rubber spatula. Add half of the flour mixture and mix on low speed just until blended. Add the rest of the flour mixture and mix just until blended. Add the chocolate chips and beat just until the chips are mixed evenly into the dough. Scrape down the bowl.

Scoop up a rounded tablespoonful of dough, then use your finger to push the dough onto 1 of the prepared cookie sheets. Repeat with the rest of the dough, spacing the mounds 3 inches apart on the cookie sheets.

When both cookie sheets are full, bake 1 cookie sheet at a time until the tops of the cookies are lightly golden in the center, 10 to 12 minutes. Ask an adult to help you remove the cookie sheet from the oven and set it on a wire rack. Let cool for 5 minutes, then use a metal spatula to move the cookies directly to the rack. Repeat to bake the rest of the cookies. Let the cookies cool completely.

Turn half of the cookies bottom side up and spread a thick layer of frosting on the surface of each upside-down cookie. Top each with a second cookie, placing the bottom side onto the filling. Serve right away.

MAKES ABOUT 40 COOKIES

Zesty Lime Cookies

Your kitchen will smell like a tropical beach when you bake these zingy cookies bursting with citrus sunshine. Add green food coloring to the glaze to make it even more lime-tastic.

COOKIES

2½ cups all-purpose flour

½ teaspoon baking powder

¼ teaspoon salt

1 cup (2 sticks) unsalted butter, at room temperature

1 cup granulated sugar

1 large egg

1 tablespoon finely grated lime zest

2 teaspoons vanilla extract

LIME ICING

2 cups powdered sugar, sifted

2 tablespoons lime juice, plus more as needed

1 tablespoon light corn syrup

Colored sugar, for sprinkling (optional)

To make the cookies, in a bowl, whisk together the flour, baking powder, and salt. In a large bowl, using an electric mixer, beat the butter and granulated sugar on medium speed until well blended, about 1 minute. Add the egg, lime zest, and vanilla and beat on low speed until combined. Turn off the mixer and scrape down the bowl with a rubber spatula. Add the flour mixture and mix just until blended. Divide the dough in half, press each piece into a disk, and wrap tightly with plastic wrap. Refrigerate until firm, at least 1 hour.

Preheat the oven to 350°F. Line 2 cookie sheets with parchment paper. Sprinkle a work surface with flour. Unwrap 1 chilled dough disk and place it on the floured surface. Using a floured rolling pin, roll out the disk to a round about ¼ inch thick. With a 2-inch round or fluted cookie cutter, cut out as many cookies as possible. Transfer to the prepared cookie sheets, spacing them 1 inch apart. Press the dough scraps into a disk, wrap in plastic wrap, and refrigerate. Repeat with the second chilled dough disk and the scraps.

Bake the cookies 1 cookie sheet at a time until lightly golden, 10 to 13 minutes. Let the cookies cool for 5 minutes, then use a metal spatula to move them directly to a wire rack. Repeat to bake the rest of the cookies. Let cool completely.

To make the icing, in a bowl, whisk together the powdered sugar, lime juice, and corn syrup until smooth. Using a spoon, drizzle the icing over the cookies, then sprinkle the icing with colored sugar, if you like. Let the icing dry for about 20 minutes and serve.

MAKES ABOUT 36 COOKIES

Chewy Coconut Macaroons

If you're a coconut lover, you'll go crazy for these chewy cookies. Made by beating egg whites into a soft, fluffy mountain, then gently folding them into mounds of shredded coconut, these macaroons are super easy to make and taste extra coconutty.

4 cups sweetened shredded coconut

1 cup sweetened condensed milk

¼ teaspoon salt

2 teaspoons vanilla extract

4 large egg whites

¼ teaspoon cream of tartar

2 tablespoons sugar

 Preheat the oven to 325°F. Line 2 cookie sheets with parchment paper and butter the paper. In a large bowl, using a fork, stir together the coconut, condensed milk, salt, and vanilla until well blended.

In a bowl, combine the egg whites and cream of tartar. Using an electric mixer, beat the egg whites on medium speed until foamy, about 1 minute. Raise the speed to medium-high and continue beating until the egg whites look shiny and smooth and they form peaks that droop when the beaters are lifted (turn off the mixer first!), 2 to 3 minutes. Continue to beat the egg whites while slowly adding the sugar, then keep beating the mixture until it holds stiff peaks when the beaters are lifted (turn off the mixer first!), about 1 minute longer.

Using a rubber spatula, gently mix half of the egg whites into the coconut mixture just until blended, then mix in the rest of the egg whites until no white streaks remain. Scoop rounded tablespoonfuls of the batter onto the prepared cookie sheets, spacing them 1½ inches apart.

Bake the macaroons 1 cookie sheet at a time until the edges and some tips of the coconut shreds are lightly browned, 15 to 17 minutes. Ask an adult to help you remove the cookie sheets from the oven and set them on a wire rack. Let cool for 5 minutes, then use a metal spatula to move the macaroons directly to the rack. Let cool completely and serve.

MAKES ABOUT 36 COOKIES

Sugar Cookies

Sugar cookies are the perfect blank canvas for pretty decorations. Cut the dough into your favorite shapes, and after baking, bedazzle the cookies with icing and sprinkles.

COOKIES

2 cups all-purpose flour

½ teaspoon baking powder

¼ teaspoon salt

½ cup (1 stick) unsalted butter, at room temperature

1 cup granulated sugar

1 large egg

1½ teaspoons vanilla extract

VANILLA ICING

2 cups powdered sugar, sifted

2 tablespoons warm water, plus more as needed

1 tablespoon light corn syrup

1 teaspoon vanilla extract

2 or 3 drops of food coloring in your favorite color(s) (optional)

Colored sugars, sprinkles, and/or candies, for decorating

 To make the cookies, in a medium bowl, whisk together the flour, baking powder, and salt. In a large bowl, using an electric mixer, beat the butter and granulated sugar on medium speed until well blended, about 1 minute. Add the egg and vanilla and beat on medium speed until combined. Turn off the mixer and scrape down the bowl with a rubber spatula. Add half of the flour mixture and mix on low speed just until blended. Add the rest of the flour mixture and mix just until blended. The dough will look lumpy, like moist pebbles. Scrape down the bowl.

Dump the dough onto a work surface and press it together into a mound. Divide the dough in half and press each piece into a disk. Wrap each disk tightly in plastic wrap and refrigerate until firm, at least 1 hour or up to overnight.

Preheat the oven to 350°F. Line 2 cookie sheets with parchment paper.

Sprinkle a clean work surface with flour. Unwrap 1 chilled dough disk and place it on the floured surface. Sprinkle the top of the dough with a little more flour. Roll out the dough with a rolling pin until it is about ¼ inch thick. Sprinkle more flour under and over the dough as needed so it doesn't stick. Using your cookie cutters, cut out as many shapes as you can, then use a metal spatula to transfer the cookies to the prepared cookie sheets, spacing them 1 inch apart. Press the dough scraps into a disk, wrap in plastic wrap, and refrigerate until firm. Repeat with the second chilled dough disk and the scraps.

Bake the cookies 1 cookie sheet at a time until the edges of the cookies are lightly browned, 10 to 12 minutes. Ask an adult to help you remove the cookie sheet from the oven and set it on a wire rack. Let cool for 10 minutes, then use a metal spatula to move the cookies directly to the rack. Let cool completely. If there is remaining dough, repeat to bake the rest of the cookies.

To make the icing, in a medium bowl, whisk together the powdered sugar, water, corn syrup, and vanilla until smooth. Add the food coloring (if using) and whisk to combine. If you're using more than 1 color, divide the icing among small bowls and make each one a different color by whisking a couple drops of food coloring into each bowl.

To decorate the cookies, using an icing spatula or a butter knife, spread icing on each cookie. While the icing is soft, decorate the cookies with colored sugars, candies, or sprinkles. Let the icing dry for about 20 minutes and serve.

MAKES ABOUT 24 COOKIES

Chocolate Crinkle Cookies

Coated in a flurry of powdered sugar and extra-fudgy inside, these cool-looking cookies will satisfy even the biggest chocolate craving. These treats also go by the name "earthquake cookies" because of their crackly tops.

½ cup powdered sugar, sifted

1⅔ cups all-purpose flour

½ cup unsweetened cocoa powder, sifted

1½ teaspoons baking powder

¼ teaspoon salt

½ cup (1 stick) unsalted butter, at room temperature

1¼ cups granulated sugar

2 large eggs

½ teaspoon vanilla extract

 Preheat the oven to 350°F. Line 2 cookie sheets with parchment paper. Put the powdered sugar into a medium bowl and set aside.

In another medium bowl, whisk together the flour, cocoa, baking powder, and salt. In a large bowl, using an electric mixer, beat the butter and granulated sugar on medium speed until fluffy and pale, about 3 minutes. Turn off the mixer and scrape down the bowl with a rubber spatula. Add 1 egg and beat on medium speed until blended. Add the other egg and the vanilla and beat until blended. Turn off the mixer and add the flour mixture. Mix on low speed just until blended. Scrape down the bowl.

Scoop up a rounded tablespoonful of dough. Scrape the dough off the spoon into the palm of your hand. Roll the dough into a ball, set it on a large plate, and shape the rest of the dough into balls in the same way.

When all of the dough has been shaped, roll the balls in the powdered sugar until completely covered. Place the balls on the prepared cookie sheets, spacing them about 2 inches apart.

Bake the cookies 1 cookie sheet at a time until crackled and puffed, 10 to 12 minutes. Ask an adult to help you remove the cookie sheet from the oven and set it on a wire rack. Let cool for 15 minutes, then use a metal spatula to move the cookies directly to the rack. Let cool completely and serve.

Double choco-rific
Make these brownie-like cookies even more chocolaty by adding ½ cup mini chocolate chips to the batter.

MAKES ABOUT 15 SANDWICHES

Ice Cream Sandwiches

What's more delicious than a bowlful of your favorite ice cream? A big, melty scoop smashed between two crispy-chewy chocolate cookies! Freeze an extra batch of the baked cookies in an airtight container so they're ready to serve anytime.

1 cup semisweet chocolate chips

½ cup (1 stick) unsalted butter

¼ cup light corn syrup

1 cup all-purpose flour

½ teaspoon baking soda

¼ teaspoon salt

⅓ cup sugar

1 large egg

1 teaspoon vanilla extract

Sprinkles, small candies, chopped toasted nuts, mini chocolate chips, or crushed cookies, for decorating

1 quart ice cream (your favorite flavor), softened for 10–15 minutes at room temperature

 Position 2 racks in the upper third of the oven so that they are evenly spaced and preheat the oven to 350°F. Line 2 cookie sheets with parchment paper.

In a saucepan, combine the chocolate chips, butter, and corn syrup. Ask an adult to help you place the pan over medium-low heat. Warm the mixture until the butter melts. Don't let the chocolate get too hot! Remove the pan from the heat and stir the chocolate mixture with a rubber spatula until it is melted and smooth. Using the rubber spatula, scrape the mixture into a large bowl and let cool. In another bowl, whisk together the flour, baking soda, and salt.

Add the sugar to the cooled chocolate mixture and stir well with a wooden spoon. Stir in the egg and vanilla until blended. Scrape down the bowl with the rubber spatula. Add the flour mixture to the chocolate mixture and stir with a wooden spoon until blended.

Scoop up a rounded tablespoonful of dough, then use your finger to push the dough onto 1 of the prepared cookie sheets. Repeat with the rest of the dough, spacing the mounds 4 inches apart on the cookie sheets. You should be able to fit 9 cookies on each cookie sheet. With your fingers, pat the mounds of dough to form 2-inch rounds so that they will spread into neat circles.

> **It's a party!**
> After you bake the cookies, set out an array of ice creams and decorations and let your friends create their own treats.

When both cookie sheets are full, bake the cookies until they puff and then begin to sink, 10 to 12 minutes. Don't overbake them, or they will become too crunchy. Ask an adult to help you remove the cookie sheets from the oven and set them on wire racks. Let cool for 15 minutes, then use a metal spatula to move the cookies directly to the racks. Let cool completely. Repeat to bake the rest of the dough.

Put the sprinkles and/or other decorations into small bowls. Turn half of the cookies bottom side up and top each with a scoop of ice cream. Place a second cookie flat side down on top of the ice cream. One at a time, pick up the ice cream sandwiches and gently press the cookies together to squish the ice cream all the way to the edges. Use a butter knife to smooth the edges, if needed. Working quickly, roll the ice cream edges in the decorations until coated all around.

Wrap each ice cream sandwich in plastic wrap and freeze until firm, at least 2 hours. Serve frozen with lots of napkins.

MAKES 12 MADELEINES

Orange Madeleines

A little freshly grated orange zest gives these adorable shell-shaped mini cakes an amazing aroma and lots of flair. The zest adds pretty orange flecks to the cakes, too.

2 large eggs

⅓ cup granulated sugar

¼ teaspoon salt

½ teaspoon vanilla extract

¼ teaspoon almond extract

1 teaspoon grated orange zest

½ cup all-purpose flour, plus more for dusting the pan

¼ cup unsalted butter, melted and cooled, plus room-temperature butter for the pan

Confectioners' (powdered) sugar for dusting

 Preheat the oven to 375°F. Using a pastry brush, coat the 12 molds of a madeleine pan with room-temperature butter, making sure you coat each and every ridge. Dust the molds with flour, tilting the pan to coat all of the surfaces. Turn the pan upside down over the kitchen sink and tap it gently to knock out the excess flour.

In a bowl, using an electric mixer, beat together the eggs, sugar, and salt on medium-high speed until light and fluffy, about 5 minutes. Beat in the vanilla and almond extracts, and the orange zest. Turn off the mixer. Sift the flour over the egg mixture and mix on low speed to incorporate. Using a rubber spatula, gently fold in one-half of the melted butter just until blended. Fold in the remaining melted butter.

Scoop a heaping tablespoonful of the batter into each mold. Bake until the tops spring back when lightly touched (ask an adult for help!), 10 to 12 minutes. Ask an adult to help you remove the pan from the oven, invert it onto a wire rack right away, and tap the pan on the rack to release the madeleines. If any of the cookies stick, use a butter knife to loosen the edges, being careful not to touch the hot pan, and invert and tap again. Use a fine-mesh sieve or a sifter, dust them with confectioners' sugar. Serve slightly warm.

MAKES 12 MADELEINES

Chocolate-Dipped Vanilla Madeleines

Sweet and fancy French madeleines are très cute when dipped into rich melted chocolate. Serve these at your next tea party. Bon appétit!

2 large eggs

⅓ cup granulated sugar

¼ teaspoon salt

1 teaspoon vanilla extract

½ cup all-purpose flour, plus more for dusting the pan

¼ cup unsalted butter, melted and cooled, plus room-temperature butter for the pan

⅓ cup semisweet chocolate chips

 Preheat the oven to 375°F. Using a pastry brush, coat the 12 molds of a madeleine pan with room-temperature butter, making sure you coat each and every ridge. Dust the molds with flour, tilting the pan to coat all of the surfaces. Turn the pan upside down over the kitchen sink and tap it gently to knock out the excess flour.

In a bowl, using an electric mixer, beat together the eggs, sugar, and salt on medium-high speed until light and fluffy, about 5 minutes. Beat in the vanilla extract. Turn off the mixer. Sift the flour over the egg mixture and mix on low speed to incorporate. Using a rubber spatula, gently fold in one-half of the melted butter just until blended. Fold in the remaining melted butter.

Scoop a heaping tablespoonful of the batter into each mold. Bake until the tops spring back when lightly touched (ask an adult for help!), 10 to 12 minutes. Ask an adult to help you remove the pan from the oven, invert it onto a wire rack right away, and tap the pan on the rack to release the madeleines. If any of the cookies stick, use a butter knife to loosen the edges, being careful not to touch the hot pan, and invert and tap again. Let cool while you melt the chocolate for dipping.

To dip the madeleines in chocolate, line a cookie sheet with parchment paper. Place the chocolate chips in a small microwave-safe bowl. Ask an adult to help you microwave the chocolate on high heat, stirring every 20 seconds, until it's melted and smooth. Don't let the chocolate get too hot! One at a time, carefully dip the wide, rounded end of each madeleine into the chocolate, then set it, shell-side up, on the prepared cookie sheet.

Refrigerate the cookies until the chocolate is set, 10 to 15 minutes. Serve. These are best eaten the same day they are baked.

A pretty gift
Chocolate-dipped madeleines are a special treat and make a memorable present for someone sweet.

Tea perfect! These sweet little cakes are ideal for an afternoon tea party. Serve them with fresh berries and fruity herbal tea.

MAKES 12 MADELEINES

Honey Madeleines

These buttery, honey-licious cakes are surprisingly easy to make. You need only a few ingredients, an electric mixer, and a shell-shaped mold. And with a little imagination, you'll feel like you're in a bakery in Paris!

5 tablespoons unsalted butter, melted and cooled

½ cup cake flour, plus more for dusting the pan

½ teaspoon baking powder

1 large egg

3 tablespoons sugar

2 tablespoons honey

2 teaspoons orange flower water

Position a rack in the lower third of the oven and preheat the oven to 400°F. Using a pastry brush and 1 tablespoon of the butter, coat the 12 molds of a madeleine pan with a thick layer of butter, making sure you coat each and every ridge. Dust the molds with flour, tilting the pan to coat all of the surfaces. Turn the pan upside down over the kitchen sink and tap it gently to knock out the excess flour.

Sift together the flour and baking powder into a bowl. In another bowl, using an electric mixer, beat together the egg and sugar on medium speed for 30 seconds. Increase the speed to high and beat until very thick and quadrupled in bulk, about 10 minutes. Add the honey and orange flower water and beat until combined. Turn off the mixer. Sprinkle the flour mixture over the egg mixture. Using a rubber spatula, gently fold in the flour mixture, then fold in the remaining 4 tablespoons butter.

Scoop a heaping tablespoonful of batter into each mold. The molds should be three-fourths full. Bake until the cookies are golden brown at the edges and the tops spring back when lightly touched (ask an adult for help!), 10 to 12 minutes. Ask an adult to help you remove the pan from the oven, invert it onto a wire rack right away, and tap the pan on the rack to release the madeleines. If any of the cookies stick, use a butter knife to loosen the edges, being careful not to touch the hot pan, and invert and tap again. Serve slightly warm. These are best eaten the same day they are baked.

MAKES 12 MADELEINES

Chocolate Madeleines

These scrumptious little chocolate cakes are perfect for baking with your friends. To make them super-duper choco-rific, dip the madeleines in melted chocolate chips following the directions on page 53.

⅓ cup all-purpose flour, plus more for dusting the pan

¼ cup unsweetened cocoa powder

2 large eggs

½ cup granulated sugar

¼ teaspoon salt

1 teaspoon vanilla extract

6 tablespoon unsalted butter, melted and cooled, plus room-temperature butter for the pan

Confectioners' (powdered) sugar for dusting

Preheat the oven to 375°F. Using a pastry brush, coat the 12 molds of a madeleine pan with room temperature butter, making sure you coat each and every ridge. Dust the molds with flour, tilting the pan to coat all of the surfaces. Turn the pan upside down over the kitchen sink and tap it gently to knock out the excess flour.

Sift together the flour and cocoa powder into a bowl. In another bowl, using an electric mixer, beat together the eggs, sugar, and salt on medium-high speed until light and fluffy, about 3 minutes. Beat in the vanilla. Turn off the mixer. Sprinkle the flour mixture over the egg mixture and mix on low speed to incorporate. Using a rubber spatula, gently fold in one-half of the melted butter just until blended. Fold in the remaining melted butter.

Scoop a heaping tablespoonful of the batter into each mold. Bake until the tops spring back when lightly touched (ask an adult for help!), about 12 minutes. Ask an adult to help you remove the pan from the oven, invert it onto a wire rack right away, and tap the pan on the rack to release the madeleines. If any of the cookies stick, use a butter knife to loosen the edges, being careful not to touch the hot pan, and invert and tap again. Use a fine-mesh sieve or a sifter, dust them with confectioners' sugar. Serve slightly warm.

MAKES 12 CUPCAKES

Pumpkin Cupcakes

Thick, tangy cream cheese frosting is the perfect topping for these delicious spiced cupcakes. Surprise your family and serve them for a winter holiday or bake them for a special autumn birthday party.

1½ cups all-purpose flour

2 teaspoons baking powder

½ teaspoon baking soda

2 teaspoons ground cinnamon

1 teaspoon ground ginger

¼ teaspoon ground nutmeg

¼ teaspoon salt

½ cup (1 stick) unsalted butter, at room temperature

⅔ cup firmly packed light brown sugar

2 large eggs

½ cup canned pumpkin puree

½ cup sour cream

Cream Cheese Frosting (page 76)

 Preheat the oven to 350°F. Line a standard 12-cup muffin pan with paper or foil liners.

In a medium bowl, whisk together the flour, baking powder, baking soda, cinnamon, ginger, nutmeg, and salt. In a large bowl, using an electric mixer, beat the butter and brown sugar on medium-high speed until fluffy, about 3 minutes. Add the eggs one at a time, beating well after adding each one. Turn off the mixer and scrape down the bowl with a rubber spatula. Add the pumpkin puree and sour cream and mix with the rubber spatula until blended. Add the flour mixture and stir with the rubber spatula just until blended. The batter will be thick.

Divide the batter evenly among the muffin cups, filling them nearly full. Bake until a wooden skewer inserted into the center of a cupcake comes out clean (ask an adult for help!), about 18 minutes. Ask an adult to help you remove the pan from the oven and set it on a wire rack. Let the cupcakes cool in the pan for 10 minutes, then lift them out and set them directly on the rack. Let cool completely.

Using a small icing spatula or a butter knife (or a piping bag), frost the cupcakes and serve.

MAKES 12 CUPCAKES

Devil's Food Cupcakes

Despite their name, these cupcakes are anything but devilish. Moist chocolate cake and rich chocolate frosting—decorated with plenty of rainbow sprinkles or other candies—are just heavenly good!

CUPCAKES

1 cup all-purpose flour

¼ cup unsweetened cocoa powder

1 teaspoon baking soda

¼ teaspoon salt

⅓ cup granulated sugar

⅓ cup firmly packed light brown sugar

4 tablespoons (½ stick) unsalted butter, at room temperature

1 large egg

1 teaspoon vanilla extract

¾ cup buttermilk

CHOCOLATE FROSTING

3½ cups powdered sugar

1 cup cocoa powder

½ cup (1 stick) unsalted butter, at room temperature

1 teaspoon vanilla extract

1 cup heavy cream

 Preheat the oven to 350°F. Line a standard 12-cup muffin pan.

To make the cupcakes, in a bowl, whisk together the flour, cocoa, baking soda, and salt. In a large bowl, using an electric mixer, beat the granulated sugar, brown sugar, and butter on medium-high speed until fluffy, about 3 minutes. Add the egg and vanilla and beat until combined. Turn off the mixer and scrape down the bowl with a rubber spatula. Add half of the flour mixture and mix on low speed just until blended. Turn off the mixer. Pour in the buttermilk and mix on low speed just until combined. Turn off the mixer. Add the rest of the flour mixture and mix just until blended. Scrape down the bowl.

Divide the batter evenly among the prepared muffin cups, filling each about three-fourths full. Bake until a wooden skewer inserted into the center of a cupcake comes out clean (ask an adult for help!), 18 to 20 minutes. Ask an adult to help you remove the pan from the oven and set it on a wire rack. Let the cupcakes cool for 10 minutes, then transfer them to the rack. Let cool.

To make the frosting, sift together the powdered sugar and cocoa into a bowl. Add the butter. Using an electric mixer, beat the mixture on low speed until crumbly. Add the vanilla and beat until combined. Turn off the mixer. Add the cream and beat until the frosting is smooth, about 1 minute. If the frosting is too thick, add more of the cream until it becomes smooth and spreadable.

Frost the cupcakes. Decorate with sprinkles or candies, if you like, and serve.

MAKES 12 CUPCAKES

White Chocolate & Raspberry Cupcakes

These sweet, berry-licious cupcakes are decorated with powdered sugar, not frosting, so they're perfect for taking on a picnic or packing in a lunchbox. If you like, you can stir in chopped strawberries or blackberries instead of raspberries.

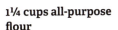

Preheat the oven to 350°F. Line a standard 12-cup muffin pan.

- 1¼ cups all-purpose flour
- 1½ teaspoon baking powder
- ⅛ teaspoon salt
- ⅔ cup granulated sugar
- 4 tablespoons (½ stick) unsalted butter, at room temperature
- 1 large egg
- 1 teaspoon vanilla extract
- ½ cup whole milk
- ½ cup white chocolate chips
- 1 cup raspberries, halved if large
- Powdered sugar, for dusting

In a medium bowl, whisk together the flour, baking powder, and salt. In a large bowl, using an electric mixer, beat the granulated sugar and butter on medium-high speed until fluffy and pale, about 3 minutes. Add the egg and vanilla and beat until combined. Turn off the mixer and scrape down the bowl with a rubber spatula. Add half of the flour mixture and mix on low speed just until blended. Turn off the mixer. Pour in the milk and mix on low speed just until combined. Turn off the mixer. Add the rest of the flour mixture and mix just until blended. Turn off the mixer. Add the white chocolate chips and stir gently with the rubber spatula, then add the raspberries and stir gently just until combined.

Divide the batter evenly among the prepared muffin cups, filling each about three-fourths full. Bake until lightly golden and a wooden skewer inserted into the center of a cupcake comes out clean (ask an adult for help!), 18 to 20 minutes. Ask an adult to help you remove the pan from the oven and set it on a wire rack. Let the cupcakes cool in the pan for 10 minutes, then lift them out and set them directly on the rack. Let cool completely.

Put the powdered sugar in a fine-mesh sieve and dust the cupcakes with sugar. Serve right away.

MAKES 24 CUPCAKES

Sweet Lemony Cupcakes

These cupcakes are sweet, tart, and perfect for enjoying in the summer sunshine. Bake up a batch or two to sell at your lemonade stand and you'll have customers coming back for more!

CUPCAKES

2¼ cups all-purpose flour

1½ teaspoons baking powder

¾ teaspoon salt

5 teaspoons poppy seeds

¾ cup (1½ sticks) unsalted butter, at room temperature

1½ cups granulated sugar

2 teaspoons finely grated lemon zest

2 large eggs

¾ cup whole milk

GLAZE

2 cups powdered sugar, sifted

3 tablespoons lemon juice

Yellow decorating sugar or white and yellow sprinkles, for decorating

 Preheat the oven to 325°F. Line 2 standard 12-cup muffin pans.

To make the cupcakes, in a bowl, whisk together the flour, baking powder, salt, and poppy seeds. In a large bowl, using an electric mixer, beat the butter, granulated sugar, and lemon zest on medium-high speed until fluffy and pale, about 3 minutes. Add the eggs one at a time, beating well after adding each one. Turn off the mixer and scrape down the bowl with a rubber spatula. Add half of the flour mixture and mix on low speed just until blended. Turn off the mixer. Pour in the milk and mix on low speed until combined. Turn off the mixer. Add the rest of the flour mixture and mix just until blended. Turn off the mixer and scrape down the bowl.

Divide the batter evenly among the muffin cups, filling each three-fourths full. Bake until golden brown and a wooden skewer inserted into the center of a cupcake comes out clean (ask an adult for help!), 18 to 20 minutes. Ask an adult to help you remove the pans from the oven and set them on wire racks. Let the cupcakes cool for 10 minutes, then transfer them to the racks. Let cool.

To make the icing, in a bowl, whisk together the powdered sugar and lemon juice. Spoon some icing on top of each cooled cupcake and use the back of the spoon to spread it to the edge. Let the icing stand for a minute, until it smooths out. While the icing is soft, sprinkle the cupcakes with the sugar or sprinkles. Don't wait too long or the icing will harden and the decorations won't stick! Let the icing dry for about 20 minutes and serve.

Frilly Fun
Decorate your cupcakes with fun, colorful toothpick flags, pinwheels, and other cute toppers.

MAKES 18 CUPCAKES

Red Velvet Cupcakes

These red velvet cupcakes have just a hint of cocoa and get their jewel-like red color from a little food coloring. Piled high with cream cheese frosting, these festive treats are ready for a party!

2 tablespoons unsweetened cocoa powder, sifted

⅓ cup boiling water

1 cup buttermilk

12 tablespoons (1½ sticks) unsalted butter, at room temperature

1½ cups sugar

3 large eggs

2 to 3 teaspoons red food coloring

2 teaspoons vanilla extract

¼ teaspoon salt

2½ cups all-purpose flour

1½ teaspoons baking soda

1 teaspoon white vinegar

Cream Cheese Frosting (page 76)

 Preheat the oven to 350°F. Line 18 cups (of two 12-cup muffin pans).

In a heatproof bowl, whisk together the cocoa and the boiling water, then whisk in the buttermilk. In a large bowl, using an electric mixer, beat the butter and sugar on medium-high speed until fluffy and pale, about 3 minutes. Add the eggs one at a time, beating well after adding each one. Add the food coloring, vanilla, and salt and beat until combined. Turn off the mixer and scrape down the bowl with a rubber spatula. Add half of the flour and beat on low speed just until blended. Turn off the mixer. Pour in the buttermilk mixture and mix on low speed just until blended. Turn off the mixer. Add the remaining flour and mix just until blended. Turn off the mixer one last time and scrape down the bowl. In a small bowl, stir together the baking soda and vinegar, then quickly stir the mixture into the batter with the rubber spatula.

Divide the batter among the prepared muffin cups, filling them about three-fourths full. Put the pans in the oven and bake until a wooden skewer inserted into the center of a cupcake comes out clean (ask an adult for help!), about 18 minutes. Ask an adult to help you remove the pans from the oven and set them on wire racks. Let the cupcakes cool in the pans for 10 minutes, then transfer them to the racks. Let cool completely.

Using a small icing spatula or a butter knife (or a piping bag), frost the cupcakes and serve.

MAKES 16 CUPCAKES

Strawberry Cheesecake Cupcakes

Swirled with sticky strawberry jam, these pretty little cheesecakes are baked in a muffin pan just like cupcakes! Try different flavors of jam, like raspberry or cherry, to mix it up.

CRUST

6 graham crackers, broken into pieces

2 teaspoons sugar

3 tablespoons unsalted butter, melted

Pinch of salt

FILLING

½ cup strawberry jam

2 (8-ounce) packages cream cheese, at room temperature

⅔ cup sugar

¼ cup sour cream

1 teaspoon vanilla extract

2 large eggs

1 tablespoon all-purpose flour

 Preheat the oven to 325°F. Line 16 cups (of two 12-cup muffin pans).

To make the crust, in the bowl of a food processor, process the graham crackers to fine crumbs. Pour the crumbs into a bowl (you should have ⅔ cup). Add the sugar, melted butter, and salt and, using a fork, stir until the crumbs are evenly moistened. Divide the mixture evenly among the prepared muffin cups (about 1 tablespoon per cup). Press the crumbs into the bottom of each cup. Bake until lightly golden, about 4 minutes. Ask an adult to help you remove the pans from the oven and set them on wire racks.

To make the filling, in the clean food processor bowl, process the jam until smooth. If the jam is very thick, add a little lemon juice or water to thin it until it is like a sauce. Scrape into a bowl and set aside. Clean the processor bowl.

In the food processor, process the cream cheese until smooth, about 3 minutes. Add the sugar and process until smooth, about 30 seconds. Scrape down the bowl. Add the sour cream and vanilla and process until combined. Add the eggs, one at a time, processing well after adding each one. Add the flour and process until combined. Scrape down the bowl and process once more.

Divide the filling evenly among the prepared muffin cups, filling each three-fourths full. Top each with a small amount of the jam, then use a toothpick to swirl the mixtures together, creating a marbled look. Bake until the cheesecakes puff and are set, about 23 minutes. Ask an adult to help you remove the pans, then let cool completely in the pans. Cover with plastic wrap and refrigerate until chilled, at least 3 hours or up to overnight. Serve.

MAKES 18 CUPCAKES

Carrot Cupcakes with Cream Cheese Frosting

Is there a better way to eat your veggies than tucked into an amazing cupcake that's topped off with ooey gooey cream cheese frosting? These are veggie-rific!

CUPCAKES

2¼ cups all-purpose flour

1 cup brown sugar

1 tablespoon baking powder

1 teaspoon cinnamon

½ teaspoon salt

1½ cups peeled and grated carrots

¾ cup vegetable oil

4 large eggs

1½ teaspoons vanilla extract

CREAM CHEESE FROSTING

1 (8-ounce) package cream cheese, at room temperature

4 tablespoons (½ stick) unsalted butter, at room temperature

2 teaspoons vanilla extract

1 cup powdered sugar

 Preheat the oven to 325°F. Line 18 cups (of two 12-cup muffin pans) with paper or foil liners.

To make the cupcakes, in a large bowl, whisk together the flour, brown sugar, baking powder, cinnamon, and salt. In a small bowl, combine the carrots, oil, eggs, and vanilla and whisk until blended. Add the carrot mixture to the flour mixture and stir with a rubber spatula just until blended.

Divide the batter evenly among the prepared muffin cups. Put the pans in the oven and bake until a wooden skewer inserted into the center of a cupcake comes out clean (ask an adult for help!), 16 to 18 minutes. Ask an adult to help you remove the pans from the oven and set them on wire racks. Let the cupcakes cool in the pans for 10 minutes, then lift them out and set them directly on the racks. Let cool completely.

To make the frosting, in a bowl, using an electric mixer, beat the cream cheese, butter, and vanilla on medium-high speed until light and fluffy, about 2 minutes. Turn off the mixer. Sift the powdered sugar through a fine-mesh sieve, ½ cup at a time, over the cream cheese mixture, then beat well after each addition. Turn off the mixer and scrape down the bowl with a rubber spatula. The frosting should be spreadable. If it's too soft, refrigerate it for about 15 minutes.

Using a small icing spatula or a butter knife, frost the cupcakes and serve.

MAKES 12 CUPCAKES

PB & J Cupcakes

Inspired by peanut butter and jelly sandwiches, these jam-filled vanilla cupcakes are topped with peanut butter frosting. Add one to your lunchbox for a sweet treat!

CUPCAKES

1¼ cups all-purpose flour

1¼ teaspoons baking powder

¼ teaspoon salt

¾ cup granulated sugar

6 tablespoons (¾ stick) unsalted butter, at room temperature

2 large eggs

1 teaspoon vanilla extract

⅓ cup whole milk

PB FROSTING

6 tablespoons (¾ stick) unsalted butter, at room temperature

¾ cup smooth peanut butter

¾ cup powdered sugar, sifted

¼ cup heavy cream

¾ cup fruit jam or preserves

 Preheat the oven to 350°F. Line a standard 12-cup muffin pan.

To make the cupcakes, in a bowl, whisk together the flour, baking powder, and salt. In another bowl, using an electric mixer, beat the granulated sugar and butter on medium-high speed until fluffy and pale, about 3 minutes. Add the eggs and vanilla and beat until combined. Turn off the mixer and scrape down the bowl with a rubber spatula. Add half of the flour mixture and mix on low speed just until blended. Turn off the mixer. Pour in the milk and mix on low speed just until combined. Turn off the mixer. Add the rest of the flour mixture and mix just until blended. Scrape down the bowl.

Divide the batter evenly among the prepared muffin cups, filling each about three-fourths full. Bake until lightly golden and a wooden skewer inserted into the center of a cupcake comes out clean (ask an adult for help!), 18 to 20 minutes. Ask an adult to help you remove the pan from the oven and set it on a wire rack. Let the cupcakes cool in the pan for 10 minutes, then transfer them to the rack. Let cool completely.

To make the frosting, in a bowl, using an electric mixer, beat the butter, peanut butter, powdered sugar, and cream on medium-low speed until smooth and combined, about 2 minutes. Ask an adult to help you use a serrated knife and halve each cupcake horizontally. Spread about 1 tablespoon of jam on each cupcake bottom, then replace the tops. Using a small icing spatula or a butter knife, frost the cupcakes and serve.

MAKES 18 CUPCAKES

S'mores Cupcakes

No campfire? No problem! Here's a way to turn everyone's favorite camping treat into delicious oven-baked goodies. These rich chocolate cupcakes are loaded with mini marshmallows and crumbled graham crackers. Yum!

1 cup all-purpose flour

¼ cup unsweetened cocoa powder, sifted

¾ teaspoon baking soda

¼ teaspoon salt

6 tablespoons (¾ stick) unsalted butter, at room temperature

½ cup granulated sugar

⅓ cup firmly packed light brown sugar

1 large egg

1 teaspoon vanilla extract

¾ cup buttermilk

⅔ cup roughly crumbled graham crackers (about 3 crackers), plus more for decorating

⅓ cup mini marshmallows, plus more for decorating

⅔ cup semisweet chocolate chips

 Preheat the oven to 350°F. Line 18 cups (of two 12-cup muffin pans).

In a medium bowl, whisk together the flour, cocoa, baking soda, and salt. In another bowl, using an electric mixer, beat the butter and sugars on medium-high speed until fluffy and pale, about 3 minutes. Add the egg and vanilla and beat until combined. Turn off the mixer and scrape down the bowl with a rubber spatula. Add half of the flour mixture and mix on low speed just until blended. Turn off the mixer. Pour in the buttermilk and mix on low speed just until combined. Turn off the mixer. Add the rest of the flour mixture and mix just until blended. Turn off the mixer. Using a rubber spatula, stir in the graham crackers and marshmallows.

Divide the batter evenly among the prepared muffin cups, filling each about two-thirds full. Bake until a wooden skewer inserted into the center of a cupcake comes out clean (ask an adult for help!), 18 to 20 minutes. Ask an adult to help you remove the pans from the oven and set them on wire racks. Let the cupcakes cool for 10 minutes, then transfer them to the racks. Let cool.

Place the chocolate chips in a small microwave-safe bowl. Ask an adult to help you microwave the chocolate on high heat, stirring every 20 seconds, until it's melted and smooth. Don't let the chocolate get too hot!

Spread a thin layer of melted chocolate on each cupcake, then top with graham crackers and marshmallows. Let the chocolate set, then serve.

MAKES 24 CUPCAKES

Black Bottom Cupcakes

There's a lot to love about these cupcakes: super chocolaty cake on the outside, creamy cheesecake on the inside, and melty chocolate chips on top. Try using a zippered plastic bag as a piping bag to fill the center of each cupcake before baking to keep things tidy.

FILLING

1 (8-ounce) package cream cheese, at room temperature

½ cup sugar

1 large egg

CUPCAKES

1½ cups cold water

½ cup vegetable oil

2 teaspoons vanilla extract

3 teaspoons balsamic vinegar

2⅓ cups all-purpose flour

½ cup unsweetened cocoa powder, sifted

1 teaspoon baking soda

1 cup sugar

½ teaspoon salt

½ cup semisweet chocolate chips

 Preheat the oven to 350°F. Line 2 standard 12-cup muffin pans with paper or foil liners.

To make the filling, in a medium bowl, using an electric mixer, beat the cream cheese, sugar, and egg on medium speed until smooth, about 2 minutes.

To make the cupcakes, in a medium bowl, combine the water, oil, vanilla, and balsamic vinegar. In a large bowl, whisk together the flour, cocoa, baking soda, sugar, and salt. Pour the wet ingredients into the flour mixture and stir with a wooden spoon until the batter is smooth (it will be runny).

Fill the muffin cups three-fourths full. Using a tablespoon measure, spoon about 1 tablespoon of the filling into the center of the batter. You will see the chocolate batter rise as the filling fills the middle. Fill all of the cupcakes.

Sprinkle the cupcakes with the chocolate chips, dividing them evenly. Put the pans in the oven and bake until a wooden skewer inserted into the center of a cupcake comes out clean (ask an adult for help!), about 25 minutes. Ask an adult to help you remove the pans from the oven and set them on wire racks. Let the cupcakes cool in the pans for 10 minutes, then lift them out and set them directly on the racks. Let cool completely and serve.

Line with color
Add personality and pizzazz to your cupcakes by using an array of liners in different colors and fun patterns.

MAKES 24 CUPCAKES

Snowball Cupcakes

These tender vanilla treats are covered in shredded coconut, so they look like fluffy snowballs—but they taste way yummier! You can color the frosting and the coconut by mixing a few drops of food coloring into each before decorating the cupcakes.

2¾ cups all-purpose flour

2 tablespoons cornstarch

1 tablespoon baking powder

⅛ teaspoon salt

1½ cups sugar

¾ cup (1½ sticks) unsalted butter, at room temperature

3 large eggs

¾ cup whole milk

½ cup water

1 tablespoon vanilla extract

Cream Cheese Frosting (page 76)

2 cups shredded sweetened coconut

 Preheat the oven to 350°F. Line two standard 12-cup muffin pans with paper or foil liners.

In a medium bowl, whisk together the flour, cornstarch, baking powder, and salt. In a large bowl, using an electric mixer, beat the sugar and the butter on medium-high speed until fluffy and pale, about 3 minutes. Add the eggs, one at a time, beating well after adding each one. Turn off the mixer and scrape down the bowl with a rubber spatula. Add the milk, water, and vanilla and beat until combined. Turn off the mixer and scrape down the bowl. Add half of the flour mixture and mix on low speed just until blended. Turn off the mixer. Add the rest of the flour mixture and mix just until blended. Scrape down the bowl.

Divide the batter evenly among the prepared muffin cups, filling them about two-thirds full. Put the pans in the oven and bake until a toothpick inserted into the center of a cupcake comes out clean (ask an adult for help!), 18 to 20 minutes. Ask an adult to help you remove the pans from the oven and set them on wire racks. Let the cupcakes cool in the pans for 10 minutes, then lift them out and set them directly on the racks. Let cool completely.

Using a small icing spatula or a butter knife, frost the cupcakes. Sprinkle them with the shredded coconut and serve.

MAKES 16 BROWNIES

Chocolate-Peanut Butter Brownies

A big pan of fudgy brownies is one of the best things to share with your friends. Creamy pools of peanut butter make these an even more delicious treats!

¾ cup (1½ sticks) unsalted butter

8 ounces semisweet chocolate, chopped into small pieces

4 large eggs

1 cup sugar

1 teaspoon vanilla extract

¼ teaspoon salt

1 cup all-purpose flour

8 tablespoons smooth peanut butter

¾ cup semisweet chocolate chips

 Preheat the oven to 350°F. Line a 9-inch square baking pan with parchment paper, extending it up and over the sides on 2 sides.

Select a saucepan and a heatproof bowl that fits snugly on top of the pan. Fill the pan one-third full of water, making sure the water doesn't touch the bottom of the bowl. Ask an adult to help you place the saucepan over medium heat. When the water is steaming, place the bowl on top of the saucepan and add the butter and chocolate to the bowl. Heat, stirring with a rubber spatula, until the mixture is melted and smooth, about 5 minutes. Don't let the chocolate get too hot! Ask an adult to help you remove the bowl from the saucepan (the bowl will be hot!) and set aside to cool slightly.

In a bowl, using an electric mixer, beat the eggs on medium speed until pale, about 4 minutes. Add the sugar, vanilla, and salt and beat until well combined. Turn off the mixer. Add the chocolate mixture and beat until blended. Turn off the mixer and scrape down the bowl with a rubber spatula. Stir in the flour with the rubber spatula just until blended.

Scrape the batter into the pan and smooth the top. Using a tablespoon measure, drop 8 dollops of peanut butter over the top, spacing them evenly. Sprinkle with the chocolate chips. Bake until a toothpick inserted into the center comes out clean (ask an adult for help!), 25 to 30 minutes. Ask an adult to help you remove the pan from the oven and put it on a wire rack. Let cool completely, then use the edges of the parchment paper to lift the brownie "cake" from the pan. Place on a cutting board and cut into 16 squares and serve.

MAKES 6 SERVINGS

Strawberry Shortcakes

Strawberry shortcakes are great for a party. Set out a plateful of tender shortcakes and bowls of sliced strawberries and whipped cream, and invite your friends to put together their own "berry" delicious desserts!

SHORTCAKES

2 cups all-purpose flour

¼ cup granulated sugar

2 teaspoons baking powder

¼ teaspoon salt

6 tablespoons (¾ stick) cold unsalted butter, cut into small cubes

¾ cup heavy cream

STRAWBERRIES

1 pound fresh strawberries

1 to 2 tablespoons granulated sugar

WHIPPED CREAM

1 cup cold heavy cream

1 tablespoon granulated sugar

1 teaspoon vanilla extract

Powdered sugar, for serving

 To make the shortcakes, preheat the oven to 375°F. Line a cookie sheet with a piece of parchment paper.

In a large bowl, whisk together the flour, granulated sugar, baking powder, and salt until evenly blended. Add the butter cubes. Using a pastry blender or 2 butter knives, cut the butter into the dry ingredients until the mixture looks like coarse crumbs, with some chunks the size of peas. Pour in the cream and stir with a wooden spoon until the dough starts to come together.

Sprinkle a work surface with flour. Turn the dough out of the bowl and onto the floured surface and pat it into a disk. Roll it out with a rolling pin, giving the disk a quarter turn now and then, into a round slab that's 1 inch thick. Pat the sides to make them neat. Use a 3-inch biscuit cutter to cut out 4 rounds. Gather the dough scraps, roll them out just as you did before, and cut out 2 more rounds.

Set the dough rounds on the prepared cookie sheet, evenly spacing them apart. Bake until the shortcakes are golden brown on top, 18 to 20 minutes. Ask an adult to help you remove the cookie sheet from the oven and set it on a wire rack. Let the shortcakes cool while you prepare the strawberries.

To prepare the strawberries, put the berries on a cutting board. Ask an adult to help you cut out the stem and core from the center of each berry and cut the berries into wedges. Put the sliced berries in a medium bowl

and sprinkle with the granulated sugar (the amount of sugar depends on how sweet the berries are—taste one!). Let the berries stand for 10 minutes.

To make the whipped cream, in a large bowl, using an electric mixer, beat the cream, granulated sugar, and vanilla on low speed until the cream begins to thicken and no longer splatters, about 2 minutes. Raise the mixer speed to medium-high and continue to beat until the cream forms peaks that droop slightly when the beaters are lifted (turn off the mixer first!), about 3 minutes.

Ask an adult to help you split each cooled shortcake in half horizontally. Place the shortcake bottoms, cut side up, on serving plates and spoon the strawberries on top, dividing them equally. Add a big spoonful of whipped cream and top with the shortcake tops. Put the powdered sugar in a fine-mesh sieve, hold it over each shortcake, and tap the side of the sieve to dust the shortcake with sugar. Serve right away.

MAKES 16 SQUARES

Rocky Road Fudge

Just like the ice cream flavor, this rocky road fudge is chock-full of marshmallows and nuts. Choose your favorite type of nut or use colored marshmallows instead of white ones. Or, just leave out the nuts and marshmallows and make good ol' plain fudge.

½ teaspoon vegetable oil

3½ cups mini marshmallows

2 cups chopped toasted walnuts, almonds, or pecans

2 cups semisweet chocolate chips

1 (14-ounce) can sweetened condensed milk

1 teaspoon vanilla extract

Line an 8-inch square baking pan with aluminum foil, gently pressing the foil into the corners and letting the extra foil hang over the sides. Soak a paper towel with the vegetable oil and use it to rub over the foil. Set aside ½ cup of the mini marshmallows and ½ cup of the nuts.

Put the chocolate chips and condensed milk in a medium microwave-safe bowl. Ask an adult to help you microwave the mixture on high for 1 minute. Stir with a rubber spatula. If the chips aren't melted, return to the microwave 1 or 2 times for 30 seconds each, stirring after each time, just until the chocolate is melted. Don't let the chocolate get too hot!

Using a rubber spatula, gently stir the vanilla, the remaining 3 cups of mini marshmallows, and the remaining 1½ cups of the nuts into the chocolate mixture. Using the spatula, scrape the chocolate mixture into the prepared baking pan. Spread it evenly and smooth the top.

Sprinkle the fudge with the reserved marshmallows and nuts and gently press them into the surface. Cover the pan with plastic wrap and refrigerate until firm, at least 30 minutes.

Holding the ends of the foil, lift the fudge out of the pan and set it on a cutting board. Peel away the foil and ask an adult to help you cut the fudge into 16 squares.

MAKES 1 LOAF

Banana-Chocolate Chip Bread

This rich, moist bread is best when you use bananas that are overly ripe, because they are a lot softer and sweeter. Chocolate chips make this an extra-special version, but you can leave them out if you like or swap them out for chopped toasted pecans.

2 cups all-purpose flour

2 teaspoons baking powder

½ teaspoon baking soda

¼ teaspoon salt

½ teaspoon ground cinnamon

⅛ teaspoon ground nutmeg

3 very ripe, large bananas, peeled and smashed

2 large eggs

1 cup firmly packed brown sugar

½ cup sour cream

1 teaspoon vanilla extract

4 tablespoons (½ stick) unsalted butter, melted

½ cup semisweet chocolate chips

Preheat the oven to 350°F. Generously butter a 9-by-5-inch loaf pan, then line it with a piece of parchment paper, extending it up and over the sides, and butter the parchment paper.

In a medium bowl, whisk together the flour, baking powder, baking soda, salt, cinnamon, and nutmeg. In a large bowl, whisk together the bananas, eggs, brown sugar, sour cream, vanilla, and butter. Add the flour mixture to the banana mixture and stir gently with a rubber spatula just until combined. Stir in the chocolate chips.

Scrape the batter into the prepared pan. Put the pan in the oven and bake until a toothpick inserted into the center of the loaf comes out clean (ask an adult for help!), about 1 hour.

Ask an adult to help you remove the pan from the oven and set it on a wire rack. Let cool in the pan for about 15 minutes, then, using the parchment, carefully lift the loaf out and place it onto the rack. Let cool completely.

Ask an adult to help you cut the bread into slices and serve.

Make muffins! Just line a 12-cup muffin pan with liners, divide the banana bread batter between the cups, and bake for 18 minutes!

Blondie sundae
For a special treat, omit the glaze and top blondie squares with vanilla ice cream, hot fudge, and sliced almonds.

MAKES 16 BLONDIES

Caramel-Glazed Blondies

Blondies are like brownies, but they have a yummy brown-sugar flavor instead of chocolate and are lighter in color. These are covered in a sweet, creamy glaze to make them even more delicious! Bake them for your next sleepover.

BLONDIES

½ cup (1 stick) unsalted butter

1 cup firmly packed dark brown sugar

1½ cups all-purpose flour

1 teaspoon baking powder

¼ teaspoon salt

2 large eggs

1 teaspoon vanilla extract

CARAMEL GLAZE

¼ cup (½ stick) unsalted butter

¾ cup firmly packed dark brown sugar

½ cup heavy cream

1 teaspoon vanilla extract

½ cup powdered sugar, sifted

 Preheat the oven to 325°F. Line a 9-inch square baking pan with parchment paper, extending it up and over the sides on two sides.

To make the blondies, in a small saucepan, combine the butter and brown sugar. Ask an adult to help you set the pan over medium heat and warm the mixture, stirring often, until melted and smooth. Using a rubber spatula, scrape the mixture into a large bowl and let cool slightly.

In a small bowl, whisk together the flour, baking powder, and salt. Add the eggs and vanilla to the butter mixture and mix with a large spoon until smooth. Add the flour mixture and stir just until combined. Pour the batter into the prepared pan. Put the pan in the oven and bake until a toothpick inserted into the center comes out with moist crumbs attached (ask an adult for help!), 20 to 25 minutes. Ask an adult to help you remove the pan from the oven and set it on a wire rack. Let cool completely.

To make the glaze, in a saucepan, combine the butter, brown sugar, and cream. Ask an adult to help you set the pan over medium heat and warm the mixture, stirring, until melted. Raise the heat to medium-high and let the mixture boil for 2 minutes. Remove from the heat, stir in the vanilla, and let cool. Stir in the powdered sugar. Spread the glaze evenly over the blondies. Let stand until set.

Holding the ends of the parchment, lift the blondies onto a cutting board. Use a warm knife to cut into 16 squares and serve.

MAKES 9 TURNOVERS

Blueberry Turnovers

You can fill these charming handheld pies with any kind of berry you like: sliced strawberries, raspberries, and blackberries all work well. They're perfect for taking on adventures because they're small and travel well.

TURNOVERS

1 sheet frozen puff pastry, thawed

2 cups blueberries

3 tablespoons granulated sugar

2 tablespoons all-purpose flour

½ teaspoon grated lemon zest

2 teaspoons lemon juice

1 large egg, lightly beaten

GLAZE

½ cup powdered sugar, sifted

1 tablespoon lemon juice

1 tablespoon orange juice

 Preheat the oven to 400°F. Line a cookie sheet with parchment paper.

To make the turnovers, unfold the puff pastry and place it on a clean work surface. Using a rolling pin, roll out the pastry to a square that's ⅛ inch thick. Cut the pastry into 3 equal strips, then cut the strips crosswise to make a total of 9 squares. Place the squares on the prepared baking sheet, spacing them apart evenly.

In a medium bowl, combine the berries, granulated sugar, flour, lemon zest, and lemon juice. Divide the berry mixture evenly among the pastry squares, placing it in the center of each square. Brush the edges of each square with the beaten egg. Fold each square on the diagonal to enclose the filling and form a triangle. Gently press along the edge with the back of the tines of a fork to seal in the filling. Put the cookie sheet in the oven and bake until the turnovers are golden brown, about 15 minutes. Ask an adult to help you remove the cookie sheet from the oven and set it on a wire rack. Let the turnovers cool completely.

To make the glaze, in a small bowl, whisk together the powdered sugar, lemon juice, and orange juice. Drizzle the glaze over the cooled turnovers. Let the glaze dry for about 15 minutes and serve.

MAKES ABOUT 16 BARS

Lemony Berry Bars

The easy press-in crust for these sweet-tart jam-filled bars is partly baked before you add the filling, to make sure that everything bakes up perfectly in the end.

CRUST

½ cup (1 stick) unsalted butter, at room temperature

1 cup all-purpose flour

¼ cup powdered sugar, sifted

1 tablespoon ice water

1 teaspoon vanilla extract

½ teaspoon salt

FILLING

¾ cup raspberry jam or other berry jam

6 large eggs

2 cups granulated sugar

¾ cup lemon juice

¼ cup all-purpose flour

¾ teaspoon baking powder

¼ teaspoon salt

½ cup powdered sugar, sifted

 Preheat the oven to 350°F. Grease a 9-inch square baking pan.

To make the crust, in a medium bowl, using an electric mixer, beat the butter on medium speed until creamy. Turn off the mixer. Add the flour, powdered sugar, ice water, vanilla, and salt and beat on low speed just until the mixture is well blended and forms small clumps that hold together when pressed between two fingers. Using clean hands, scoop the dough into the prepared pan and press to form an even layer in the bottom of the pan. Refrigerate for 10 minutes.

Put the pan in the oven and bake the crust until golden, about 15 minutes. Ask an adult to help you remove the pan from the oven and set it on a wire rack. Reduce the oven temperature to 325°F.

To make the filling, using a rubber spatula, ask an adult to help you carefully spread the jam evenly over the warm crust. In a medium bowl, whisk the eggs, granulated sugar, lemon juice, flour, baking powder, and salt until well combined. Pour the egg mixture over the jam-topped crust, carefully spreading it with the spatula to form an even layer.

Return the pan to the oven and bake until the filling doesn't jiggle when you gently shake the pan (ask an adult for help!), 40 to 45 minutes. Ask an adult to help you remove the pan from the oven and set it on a wire rack. Let cool, then transfer to the refrigerator to cool completely. Ask an adult to help you cut around the edges of the pan to loosen the sides; then cut the bars into small rectangles or squares. Just before serving, put the powdered sugar in a fine-mesh sieve and dust the bars with sugar.

MAKES ABOUT 25 TRUFFLES

Chocolate Truffles

If you love chocolate, these super choco-licious candies are for you! To give them as sweet little gifts to friends and family, put the truffles in colorful plastic bags and tie the bags with pretty ribbons or tuck them into candy cups and nestle them in a pretty box.

¼ cup heavy cream

4 tablespoons (½ stick) unsalted butter, cut into small pieces

8 ounces semisweet chocolate, chopped into small pieces

¼ teaspoon vanilla extract

¼ cup powdered sugar or unsweetened cocoa powder, sifted

 In a saucepan over medium heat, warm the cream until tiny bubbles appear around the edges of the pan (ask an adult to help!). Turn off the heat. Add the butter and chocolate to the saucepan and stir with a rubber spatula until everything is melted and the mixture is smooth. If the chocolate doesn't seem to be melting, turn on the heat to medium and warm, stirring, just until the mixture is smooth. Don't let the mixture get too hot!

Let the mixture cool for about 15 minutes. Using the rubber spatula, stir in the vanilla and scrape the mixture into a shallow bowl. Cover the bowl with plastic wrap and refrigerate until the chocolate mixture is solid, at least 4 hours or overnight.

Using a melon baller, scoop the chocolate mixture to make rough balls the size of a gumball. (The mixture will be rather firm, so you may want to ask an adult to help with scooping.) Place each scoop of truffle mixture onto a large plate.

Put the powdered sugar or cocoa in a shallow bowl. (Powdered sugar will give the truffles an extra layer of sweetness. Cocoa will make the truffles intensely chocolaty.) Working with 1 truffle scoop at a time, use the palms of your hands to roll it into a smooth, round ball and return the ball to the plate. After rolling, put the balls in the bowl with the coating of your choice. Roll each truffle in the powdered sugar or cocoa until it is completely coated, then put in a serving dish. Cover and store the truffles in the refrigerator until you are ready to eat them or offer them.

MAKES 12 TARTLETS

Raspberry-Chocolate Tartlets

As cute as they are delicious, these dainty mini tarts are perfect for a tea party. The tartlet shells are baked in a muffin pan, then each one is layered with raspberry jam, melt-in-your-mouth chocolate, and fresh raspberries.

TARTLET SHELLS

1 large egg yolk

3 tablespoons ice water

1 teaspoon vanilla extract

1¼ cups all-purpose flour

¼ cup granulated sugar

⅛ teaspoon salt

½ cup (1 stick) cold unsalted butter, cut into small pieces

FILLING

4 ounces semisweet chocolate, chopped

3 tablespoons unsalted butter

1 tablespoon light corn syrup

¼ cup raspberry jam

2 cups raspberries

Powdered sugar, for dusting (optional)

 To make the tartlet shells, in a small bowl, whisk the egg yolk, ice water, and vanilla until combined. In a food processor, pulse together the flour, granulated sugar, and salt. Scatter the butter pieces over the dry ingredients and pulse until the mixture resembles coarse cornmeal. Add the egg yolk mixture and pulse just until the dough clumps together.

Transfer the dough to a clean work surface, pat it into a ball with your hands, and flatten into a disk. Wrap the disk tightly in plastic wrap and refrigerate until chilled and firm, at least 30 minutes or up to overnight.

Spray the cups of a standard 12-cup muffin pan with nonstick cooking spray.

Sprinkle a clean work surface with flour. Unwrap the dough disk and place it on the floured surface. Sprinkle the top of the dough with a little more flour. Flour a rolling pin and roll out the dough until it is about ⅛ inch thick. Sprinkle more flour under and over the dough as needed so it doesn't stick. Using a 4-inch round cookie cutter, cut out as many rounds as you can from the dough. Press the dough scraps together, re-roll, and cut out additional rounds. You should have a total of 12 rounds. Line each cup of the prepared muffin pan with a dough round, easing it in, then patting firmly into the bottom and up the sides of the cup. Once you've lined all the cups, freeze the tartlet shells in the pan until firm, about 30 minutes.

~ *Continued on page 110* ~

Choco-cream pie

For sweet little cream tartlets, omit the jam and fresh fruit, fill the tartlets as directed, and top each with whipped cream.

~ *Continued from page 109* ~

Place an oven rack in the lower third of the oven and preheat the oven to 375°F.

Place the pan in the oven and bake the tartlet shells until golden brown, about 15 minutes. Ask an adult to help you remove the pan from the oven and set it on a wire rack. Let cool completely, then carefully lift out the tartlet shells and set them on a large, flat serving plate to cool.

To make the filling, combine the chocolate, butter, and corn syrup in a medium microwave-safe bowl. Ask an adult to help you microwave the mixture on high heat, stirring every 20 seconds until it's melted and smooth. Don't let the chocolate mixture get too hot!

Spread ½ teaspoon of raspberry jam in the bottom of each cooled tartlet shell. Spoon in the chocolate mixture, dividing it evenly. Let the tartlets stand at room temperature to allow the chocolate to set, 1 to 2 hours.

Top each tartlet with raspberries. If you like, put some powdered sugar into a fine-mesh sieve, hold the sieve over the tartlets, and tap the side of the sieve to dust the tartlets with sugar. Serve right away.

MAKES 8–10 SERVINGS

Easy Cheesecake Pie

Who doesn't love smooth, creamy cheesecake in a crunchy graham cracker crust? Topped off with fresh, colorful berries (or other ripe summer fruit), this easy-to-make pie is perfect for a summertime party.

CRUST

15 graham crackers, broken into pieces

4 tablespoons (½ stick) unsalted butter, melted

3 tablespoons sugar

¼ teaspoon ground cinnamon

FILLING

2 (8-ounce) packages cream cheese, at room temperature

1 (14-ounce) can sweetened condensed milk

1 teaspoon finely grated lemon zest

3 tablespoons lemon juice

Mixed berries, for decorating (optional)

Preheat the oven to 350°F. Put the graham crackers in a zippered plastic bag. Press out the air and seal the bag. Use a rolling pin to crush the crackers into fine crumbs, pounding them lightly or using a gentle back-and-forth rolling motion. Measure out 1¼ cups of crumbs.

To make the crust, in a bowl, combine the graham cracker crumbs, melted butter, sugar, and cinnamon. Stir with a wooden spoon until the crumbs are evenly moistened. Pour the crumb mixture into a 9-inch glass pie dish. Using your hands, press the crumbs into an even layer into the bottom and all the way up the sides of the dish. Put the pie dish in the oven and bake until the crust is firm, 6 to 7 minutes. Ask an adult to help you remove the pie dish from the oven and place it on a wire rack. Let cool completely, about 30 minutes.

To make the filling, in a large bowl, using an electric mixer, beat the cream cheese on medium speed until smooth, 2 to 3 minutes. Turn off the mixer. Add the condensed milk and beat until smooth, about 1 minute. Turn off the mixer and scrape down the bowl with a rubber spatula. Add the lemon zest and juice and beat until the mixture is smooth, about 30 seconds. Using the rubber spatula, scrape the filling into the cooled piecrust. Spread the filling out evenly and smooth the top. Refrigerate the pie until well chilled, about 3 hours.

If you like, top the pie with mixed berries. Ask an adult to help you cut the pie into wedges and serve.

MAKES 8 SERVINGS

Apple Oven Pancake

Unlike pancakes that you make on the stovetop, this is one big puffy pancake that bakes in the oven. Have an adult help you pour the batter over the apples in the hot pan, then watch through the oven door as the pancake puffs up like magic!

1 large baking apple, such as Gala or Granny Smith

4 tablespoons granulated sugar

½ teaspoon ground cinnamon

3 large eggs

1 cup whole milk

¾ cup all-purpose flour

¾ teaspoon vanilla extract

2 tablespoons powdered sugar

 Preheat the oven to 400°F. Butter a 9-inch glass pie dish.

Ask an adult to help you peel the apple, cut it into quarters, and remove the core from each quarter. Cut the apple quarters into small chunks.

In a medium bowl, using a fork, stir together 2 tablespoons of the granulated sugar and ¼ teaspoon of the cinnamon. Add the apple chunks and toss with the fork until the pieces are evenly coated with the cinnamon-sugar. Transfer the apple chunks to the prepared dish, spreading them out evenly with the fork.

In a blender, combine the remaining granulated sugar, the remaining cinnamon, the eggs, milk, flour, and vanilla. Put the lid on securely and blend on medium speed until the ingredients are well mixed and frothy, about 1 minute.

Put the pie dish in the oven and bake the apple chunks for 5 minutes. Ask an adult to help you pull out the oven rack just enough so that you can pour the batter evenly over the apples. Carefully slide the rack back into the oven and close the oven door. Bake the pancake until puffed and brown, about 25 minutes.

Ask an adult to help you remove the dish from the oven and set it on a wire rack. While the pancake is still warm, put the powdered sugar in a fine-mesh sieve. Hold the sieve over the pancake and dust the pancake with sugar. Ask an adult to help you cut the pancake into wedges and serve.

MAKES 6 SERVINGS

Cherry Crisp

A crisp is a baked fruit dessert with a sweet, crunchy topping of oats, flour, and sugar. This crisp is delicious on its own, but vanilla ice cream makes it totally irresistible!

TOPPING

4 tablespoons (½ stick) unsalted butter, at room temperature

¼ cup firmly packed light brown sugar

½ teaspoon ground cinnamon

Pinch of salt

½ cup old-fashioned oats

¼ cup all-purpose flour

FILLING

2 pounds frozen pitted cherries, thawed

1 teaspoon vanilla extract

½ cup granulated sugar

1 tablespoon cornstarch

Pinch of salt

Vanilla ice cream, for serving

 To make the topping, in a medium bowl, using a wooden spoon, stir together the butter, brown sugar, cinnamon, and salt until combined. Stir in the oats and flour. Cover with plastic wrap and refrigerate while you make the filling.

Preheat the oven to 375°F. Butter a 2-quart glass baking dish.

To make the filling, set a colander over a bowl and put the cherries in the colander to drain off any liquid. Put the drained cherries in a large bowl, add the vanilla, and stir with a wooden spoon. Sprinkle in the granulated sugar, cornstarch, and salt and stir to combine.

Transfer the cherry mixture to the prepared baking dish and spread it out evenly. Remove the topping from the refrigerator and sprinkle it evenly over the fruit. Put the dish in the oven and bake, until the filling is bubbling and the topping is brown, 30 to 35 minutes.

Ask an adult to help you remove the dish from the oven and set it on a wire rack to cool for about 20 minutes.

To serve, scoop up portions of the warm crisp onto dessert plates. Top each serving with ice cream and serve right away.

MAKES 8–10 SERVINGS

Golden Layer Cake with Chocolate Frosting

This towering chocolate-frosted vanilla butter cake will make your friends and family say, "Wow!" Decorate it with your favorite colored sprinkles for a birthday, write a fun message on top with icing, or mound fresh raspberries onto the center.

CAKE

3 cups all-purpose flour

2 teaspoons baking powder

½ teaspoon salt

1 cup (2 sticks) unsalted butter, at room temperature

2 cups granulated sugar

4 large eggs

1 cup buttermilk

FROSTING

2 cups semisweet chocolate chips

½ cup (1 stick) unsalted butter, at room temperature

1 cup sour cream

2 teaspoons vanilla extract

5 cups powdered sugar, sifted

Sprinkles and/or candies, for decorating

 Preheat the oven to 350°F. Trace the bottom of two 8-inch round cake pans onto sheets of parchment paper and cut out the circles with scissors. Rub the insides of the cake pans with a little butter. Put the paper circles in the bottom of the pans and butter the paper.

To make the cake, in a medium bowl, whisk together the flour, baking powder, and salt. In a large bowl, using an electric mixer, beat the butter and granulated sugar on medium-high speed until fluffy and pale, 3 to 4 minutes. Turn off the mixer and scrape down the bowl with a rubber spatula. Add 2 of the eggs to the butter mixture and beat on medium speed until well combined. Turn off the mixer. Add the remaining 2 eggs and beat on medium speed until well combined. Turn off the mixer and scrape down the bowl. Add half of the flour mixture and mix on low speed just until blended. Turn off the mixer. Pour in the buttermilk and mix on low speed just until blended. Turn off the mixer. Add the remaining flour mixture and mix just until blended. Turn off the mixer one last time and scrape down the bowl.

Divide the batter evenly between the cake pans and gently smooth the tops with the rubber spatula. Put the cake pans in the oven and bake until the cakes are golden brown and a wooden skewer inserted into the centers of the cakes comes out clean (ask an adult for help!), 45 to 50 minutes.

~ Continued on page 119 ~

~ *Continued from page 116* ~

Ask an adult to help you remove the cake pans from the oven and set them on wire racks. Let cool for 20 minutes, then run a table knife around the inside edge of each cake pan. Turn the pans over onto the racks. Lift away the pans and the parchment paper and let the cakes cool completely, upside down, about 2 hours.

To make the frosting, put the chocolate chips in a microwave-safe bowl. Ask an adult to help you microwave the chips on high heat, stirring every 20 seconds until they are melted and smooth. Don't let the chocolate get too hot!

In a large bowl, using the electric mixer, beat the butter, sour cream, and vanilla until smooth. Add the melted chocolate and beat until smooth. With the electric mixer on low speed, beat in the powdered sugar ½ cup at a time. When all of the sugar has been added, raise the speed to high and beat until the frosting is nice and smooth. Scrape down the bowl with the spatula and beat for 1 minute more.

When the cakes have cooled, place one layer on a cake stand or plate. Using an offset spatula, spread some of the frosting over the top, nearly to the edge, making a thick layer as even as possible. Place the second cake layer on top of the frosting, trying to line up the sides of the cakes. Spread more frosting over the top of the cake and down the sides, creating a thick layer. Decorate the cake with sprinkles and/or candies.

Serve the cake right away or cover it loosely with plastic wrap and refrigerate for up to 3 days. Ask an adult to help you cut the cake into wedges for serving.

> **Cake 'n' ice cream**
> *Serve slices of the cake with big scoops of your favorite ice cream for an extra-special treat!*

Index

A
Apple Oven Pancake, 112

B
Baking tips and hints
    basic baking tools, 12
    help from adults, 8
    safety tips, 11
Banana–Chocolate Chip Bread, 96
Bars
    Caramel-Glazed Blondies, 99
    Chocolate–Peanut Butter Brownies, 89
    Lemony Berry Bars, 105
Berries
    Blueberry Turnovers, 100
    Raspberry-Chocolate Tartlets, 109
    Strawberry Shortcakes, 90
    White Chocolate & Raspberry Cupcakes, 69
Black Bottom Cupcakes, 80
Blondies, Caramel-Glazed, 99
Blueberry Turnovers, 100
Bread, Banana–Chocolate Chip, 96
Brownies, Chocolate–Peanut Butter, 89

C
Cakes. *See also* Cupcakes
    Golden Layer Cake with Chocolate Frosting, 116
Candy
    Chocolate Truffles, 106
    Rocky Road Fudge, 95
Caramel-Glazed Blondies, 99
Carrot Cupcakes with Cream Cheese Frosting, 76
Cheesecake Pie, Easy, 111
Cherry Crisp, 115
Chewy Coconut Macaroons, 37
Chocolate
    Banana–Chocolate Chip Bread, 96
    Black Bottom Cupcakes, 80
    Chocolate Chip Cookie Sandwiches, 33
    Chocolate Crinkle Cookies, 42
    Chocolate-Dipped Vanilla Madeleines, 52
    Chocolate Frosting, 64, 116
    Chocolate Madeleines, 58
    Chocolate–Peanut Butter Brownies, 89
    Chocolate Truffles, 106
    Chocolate Whoopie Pies, 20
    Devil's Food Cupcakes, 64
    Ice Cream Sandwiches, 44
    Raspberry-Chocolate Tartlets, 109
    Red Velvet Cupcakes, 73
    Rocky Road Fudge, 95
    S'mores Cupcakes, 79
    White Chocolate & Raspberry Cupcakes, 69
Cinnamon
    Snickerdoodles, 25
Coconut
    Chewy Coconut Macaroons, 37
    Snowball Cupcakes, 83
Cookie cutters, 12
Cookies
    Chewy Coconut Macaroons, 37
    Chocolate Chip Cookie Sandwiches, 33
    Chocolate Crinkle Cookies, 42
    Chocolate Whoopie Pies, 20
    Elephant Ears, 26
    Ice Cream Sandwiches, 44
    Lemony Cookie Flower Pops, 29
    Pinwheel Icebox Cookies, 23
    Snickerdoodles, 25
    Sugar Cookies, 38
    Thumbprint Cookies, 19
    Zesty Lime Cookies, 34
Cookie sheets, 12
Cream cheese
    Black Bottom Cupcakes, 80
    Cream Cheese Frosting, 76
    Easy Cheesecake Pie, 111
    Strawberry Cheesecake Cupcakes, 74
Crisp, Cherry, 115
Cupcakes
    Black Bottom Cupcakes, 80
    Carrot Cupcakes with Cream Cheese Frosting, 76
    Devil's Food Cupcakes, 64
    PB & J Cupcakes, 77
    Pumpkin Cupcakes, 63
    Red Velvet Cupcakes, 73
    S'mores Cupcakes, 79
    Snowball Cupcakes, 83
    Strawberry Cheesecake Cupcakes, 74

Sweet Lemony Cupcakes, 70
White Chocolate & Raspberry Cupcakes, 69

D
Devil's Food Cupcakes, 64

E
Easy Cheesecake Pie, 111
Electric appliances, safety tips for, 11
Electric mixers, 12
Elephant Ears, 26

F
Frostings
  Chocolate Frosting, 64, 116
  Cream Cheese Frosting, 76
  PB Frosting, 77
Fruit jam or preserves
  Lemony Berry Bars, 105
  PB & J Cupcakes, 77
  Raspberry-Chocolate Tartlets, 109
  Strawberry Cheesecake Cupcakes, 74
  Thumbprint Cookies, 19
Fudge, Rocky Road, 95

G
Glazes
  for Blueberry Turnovers, 100
  Caramel Glaze, 99
  Lemon Glaze, 70

Golden Layer Cake with Chocolate Frosting, 116
Graham crackers
  Easy Cheesecake Pie, 111
  S'mores Cupcakes, 79
  Strawberry Cheesecake Cupcakes, 74

H
Honey Madeleines, 57

I
Icebox Cookies, Pinwheel, 23
Ice Cream Sandwiches, 44
Icings
  Lemon Icing, 29
  Lime Icing, 34
  Vanilla Icing, 38
Icing spatulas, 12

L
Lemon
  Lemon Glaze, 70
  Lemon Icing, 29
  Lemony Berry Bars, 105
  Lemony Cookie Flower Pops, 29
  Sweet Lemony Cupcakes, 70
Lime
  Lime Icing, 34
  Zesty Lime Cookies, 34

M
Macaroons, Chewy Coconut, 37
More Treats
  Apple Oven Pancake, 112
  Banana–Chocolate Chip Bread, 96
  Blueberry Turnovers, 100
  Caramel-Glazed Blondies, 99
  Cherry Crisp, 115
  Chocolate–Peanut Butter Brownies, 89
  Chocolate Truffles, 106
  Easy Cheesecake Pie, 111
  Golden Layer Cake with Chocolate Frosting, 116
  Lemony Berry Bars, 105
  Raspberry-Chocolate Tartlets, 109
  Rocky Road Fudge, 95
  Strawberry Shortcakes, 90
Madeleine pans, 12
Madeleines
  Chocolate-Dipped Vanilla Madeleines, 52
  Chocolate Madeleines, 58
  Honey Madeleines, 57
  Orange Madeleines, 51
Marshmallows
  Chocolate Whoopie Pies, 20
  Rocky Road Fudge, 95
  S'mores Cupcakes, 79
Muffin pans, 12

N
Nuts
  Rocky Road Fudge, 95

O

Orange Madeleines, 51
Oven mitts, 12
Oven Pancake, Apple, 112
Oven safety tips, 11

P

Pancake, Apple Oven, 112
Parchment paper, 12
PB & J Cupcakes, 77
Peanut butter
    Chocolate–Peanut Butter
        Brownies, 89
    PB Frosting, 77
    PB & J Cupcakes, 77
Pie, Easy Cheesecake, 111
Pinwheel Icebox Cookies, 23
Puff pastry
    Blueberry Turnovers, 100
    Elephant Ears, 26
Pumpkin Cupcakes, 63

R

Raspberries
    Raspberry-Chocolate Tartlets, 109
    White Chocolate & Raspberry
        Cupcakes, 69
Raspberry jam
    Lemony Berry Bars, 105
    Raspberry-Chocolate Tartlets, 109
    Thumbprint Cookies, 19
Red Velvet Cupcakes, 73
Rocky Road Fudge, 95
Rubber spatulas, 12

S

Shortcakes, Strawberry, 90
S'mores Cupcakes, 79
Snickerdoodles, 25
Snowball Cupcakes, 83
Spatulas, for icing, 12
Spatulas, rubber, 12
Strawberry Cheesecake
    Cupcakes, 74
Strawberry Shortcakes, 90
Sugar Cookies, 38
Sweet Lemony Cupcakes, 70

T

Tartlets, Raspberry-Chocolate, 109
Thumbprint Cookies, 19
Truffles, Chocolate, 106
Turnovers, Blueberry, 100

V

Vanilla
    Chocolate-Dipped Vanilla
        Madeleines, 52
    Vanilla Icing, 38

W

Whipped Cream, 90
White Chocolate & Raspberry
    Cupcakes, 69
Whoopie Pies, Chocolate, 20

Z

Zesty Lime Cookies, 34

weldon**owen**

1150 Brickyard Cove Road, Richmond, CA 94801
www.weldonowen.com

WELDON OWEN INTERNATIONAL
President & Publisher Roger Shaw
VP, Sales & Marketing Amy Kaneko
Finance Manager Philip Paulick

Associate Publisher Amy Marr
Project Editor Kim Laidlaw
Associate Editor Emma Rudolph

Creative Director Kelly Booth
Designer Alexandra Zeigler
Production Designer Monica S. Lee

Production Director Chris Hemesath
Associate Production Director Michelle Duggan

Photographer Nicole Hill Gerulat
Food Stylists Tara Bench, Robyn Valarik
Prop Stylists Veronica Olson, Leigh Noe
Hair & Makeup Kathy Hill

AMERICAN GIRL *BAKING*
Conceived and produced by Weldon Owen, Inc.
In collaboration with Williams Sonoma, Inc.
3250 Van Ness Avenue, San Francisco, CA 94109

A WELDON OWEN PRODUCTION
Copyright © 2015 Weldon Owen International,
Williams Sonoma, Inc., and American Girl

All rights reserved, including the right of reproduction in whole or in part in any form.

All American Girl marks are owned by and used under license from American Girl.

Library of Congress Cataloging in Publication data is available

ISBN 13: 978-1-68188-649-7

10 9 8 7 6 5 4 3 2 1
2024 2023 2022 2021 2020

Printed in China

ACKNOWLEDGMENTS

Weldon Owen wishes to thank the following people for their generous support
to help produce this book: Laura Bee, Marie Bench, Mary Bench, David Bornfriend,
Peggy Fallon, Amy Machnak Hash, Taylor Olson, A'Lissa Olson, Abby Stolfo, and Cassidy Tuttle

A VERY SPECIAL THANK YOU TO:

Our models: Avenlie Fullmer, Abigail Holtby, Sophia Jarque,
Swayzie King, Jane Robinson, Eden Rosenthal, and Kaia Sperry

Our locations: The Copes, The Williamsons, and The Wilsons

Our party resources: Oh Happy Day Shop, Shop Sweet Lulu, and Sweetapolita

Our clothing resources: Rachel Riley (rachelriley.com) and Tea Collection (teacollection.com)